Praise for Ron Missun and *Hol*

"Missun conveys a lot of specific information in fewer than 250 pages, but the strongest aspect of his book, by far, is its consistently compassionate tone. He never comes across as being solely driven by numbers; rather, his tone is that of a friendly confidante who happens to be very knowledgeable about finance."

— KIRKUS REVIEWS

"Missun takes a refreshing detour by urging readers to 'rethink' their retirement plan, keeping 'matters of the heart' at the forefront. He includes all the conventional advice—the nuts-and-bolts of personal finance, setting up emergency funds, portfolio management—but also delves into the why behind retirement planning, emphasizing how to uncover cognitive blind spots that may derail investment strategies and stressing that 'investing early and often is essential.' Beyond the day-to-day grind of retirement planning, Missun urges readers to make a positive mark on loved ones and the world at large."

—BOOKLIFE

"*Holistic Retirement Planning* lives up to its name. If utilized effectively, it can significantly alter the course of your life. Ron Missun's exhaustive exploration of the subject leaves readers well-informed and eager to learn more. His reassuring message is clear: no matter your current life stage, it's never too late to start planning for retirement."

— LITERARY TITAN

holistic
RETIREMENT PLANNING

BEING INTENTIONAL WITH
heart, mind, and money
AT ANY AGE

RON MISSUN, PHD, CRPC™

Printed in the United States of America.
First edition 2024.

Cover and layout design by G Sharp Design, LLC.
www.gsharpmajor.com

Library of Congress Control Number: 9798990890107

ISBN 979-8-9908901-0-7 (paperback)
ISBN 979-8-9908901-3-8 (hardcover)
ISBN 979-8-9908901-1-4 (ebook)
ISBN 979-8-9908901-2-1 (audiobook)

Disclaimer

This book is for retirement planning education only. No opinion or information contained in this book is personal advice or should be taken as such. Retirement planning depends on one's situation and is different for everyone. Consult a professional for personal advice.

While the opinions and information in this book are believed to be true and accurate as of the publication date, neither the author, editor, nor publisher can accept any legal responsibility for any errors or omissions made. They make no warranty, express or implied, for the material contained within.

Trademarked names, logos, or images may appear in this book. The trademark symbol may not appear with every occurrence of a trademarked name, logo, or image. I use the names, logos, and images only in an editorial fashion and to the benefit of the trademark owner with no intention of infringement of the trademark.

Holistic Retirement Planning presents calculations from two sources. One source is historical data from Dr. Aswath Damodaran, a professor of finance at the Stern School of Business at New York University. The other is FIRECalc, an online calculator. Any opinions expressed in this book are those of the author. Dr. Damodaran and the creator and owner of FIRECalc do not necessarily hold the same opinions as the author.

To My Family

I DEDICATE THIS book to my father, Henry Missun. I learned how important family is by witnessing how he conducted his life. He never had a high-paying job but retired at an early age without the benefit of a company pension. My father was interested in personal finance and educated himself on investing. I believe he would have pursued a job in finance if he had the opportunities my brother and I had. Dad passed away in 2017. My thoughts of him persist and his wise words are fondly remembered. I will release *Holistic Retirement Planning* on his birthday to honor his influence on my life and his passion for personal finance.

I grew up with two incredible parents. Mom, thank you for everything you have done and continue to do for me. You are the yardstick I use to measure the decency in other people. Few come close to the standard you live your life by. I appreciate the love, advice, and support I received from you over my lifetime. As a child, it was apparent that you and Dad valued education. Thank you for investing in my future and making it a priority. It is remarkable to call a parent one of your closest friends, but I cherish our relationship and love you more than I can express. Oh, one last thing. I must thank you and Dad for not naming me Peter or Richard. Grade school would have been brutal!

Finally, to my older and sometimes wiser brother, Bob: Your influence on my life surpasses that of anyone else. You were a primary role model for me as a child and my sense of humor has your stamp all over it. I have learned and continue to discover a lot from you—the way you handled adversity since becoming a paraplegic is inspiring. Some who know we share a home believe I am providing care for you but when I hear that, I correct them. I receive something far more valuable in exchange for my help with small matters. You are not just my brother, you are my best friend and are always there for me. Love you, buddy!

Table of Contents

Preface

THE LOSS OF a spouse, whether through death or divorce, can be a significant life stressor. My divorce was challenging but it also became a catalyst for profound personal growth. I realized I had been merely existing and reacting to life's circumstances rather than living with intention. This awakening sparked a desire for change, a commitment to improve my quality of life, and a newfound appreciation for the beauty of life itself.

Seeking ways to change required more intention than ever before. Suddenly single, I needed to scrutinize my values and personal goals. Shortly after my divorce in 2019, I had plenty of time for self-examination—contemplating my values, goals, and purpose during lockdown was fruitful. I have since made time for reflection a routine part of my life.

These life experiences compelled me to write *Holistic Retirement Planning*. I realized one of my purposes was to enhance the lives of others. Sharing my experiences and the methods I used to examine my values, goals, and purpose might be one way to do that. Since few are well versed in personal finance or the services and costs associated with financial advisors, I decided to write a book that addressed personal and financial planning with examples from my life.

I pondered what topics to include in a holistic retirement planning book. Matters of the heart, including goals, values, and purpose, should be the focal point of any retirement plan. Our brain can help us better understand our goals and values and learn about financial matters. Is our brain perfect? No, it is not. Emotions, blind spots, and biases can all cause poor decision-making. I decided that mitigating the limitations of the brain—a topic most retirement planning books ignore—was essential. It is best to address the heart and mind before considering personal finance.

Each of us is at a different stage on this holistic journey. Some may have recently retired while others may be close and seek insight into a transition phase. Then there are those who are young and eager to plan for retirement early—a group I applaud for such proactive efforts. Commitment to early planning is a testament to foresight and determination.

Another perspective on a journey's progress involves assessing the level of financial and non-financial preparation for retirement. People often show higher proficiency in one area over another. My relative strength has been the financial side, but I am working hard to enhance my non-financial preparation. We are all a work in progress with room for improvement.

Wherever you may be, this book will offer something of value. I invite you to approach the material earnestly and wish you well on your journey.

Introduction

WOULD YOU LIKE some do-overs? Most individuals experience regret concerning decisions they made or failed to make in their lifetime. Some may wish to return to July 2010 and purchase 10,000 shares of Tesla for $1.28 per share, but I am talking about something else. What about the sound financial decisions we did not make because of a lack of awareness, education, or interest? For example, later in this book, I discuss my foolish spending patterns as a teenager. I was not thinking about how I might judge my spending decisions 40 years later. The actual cost of instant gratification was never contemplated.

The do-overs go beyond financial choices. They also pertain to life decisions; how we spend our time and who we spend it with. Does our life reflect well on our values and desires? Did any missteps or neglect cause a rift in our relationships with others? I spend more time thinking about these questions now than 10 years ago. Maybe it's just me, but I suspect older people reflect on their lives more often. Constructive reflection is a good thing.

Given the opportunity to travel back in time, what advice would I offer my 16-year-old self before starting part-time work at Target? That advice is below.

1. Regularly consider values and goals to experience fewer regrets in life.
2. Dedicate more time to daily self-reflection.
3. Prioritize creating lasting memories with loved ones.

Several events affected my life; the first two happened just a few months apart. I discuss the first event in Chapter 1. The second event occurred on March 17, 1990. On that day, I received two pieces of news: 1) I was being accepted into the PhD program in economics at the University of Illinois. I was elated! 2) I learned that my best friend had passed away after losing his battle with leukemia. Ever since then, my mind has tied these two events together. Graduate school was a time of change and facing new and complex challenges. When the going got tough, I became driven. My best friend never could live out his dreams, so I was determined to live out mine. I thought of him during my deepest lows and moments of triumph. I often ponder how my life would be different if he were still here.

Cherish family and close friends who have your back—your values and goals should reflect that. Even scientific evidence shows that making these relationships a focal point is beneficial! Solid and caring relationships impact your happiness, health, and longevity. If you have yet to experience the TED talk on happiness by Dr. Robert Waldinger, I recommend investing 13 minutes of your life to become one of the over 47 million people who have seen it because it is excellent and valuable.[1] If you want to learn more after you watch it, I recommend *The Good Life*, a book he co-authored with Marc Schulz in 2023. It is an excellent read!

---

1   Robert Waldinger: What makes a good life? Lessons from the longest study on happiness | TED Talk. https://www.ted.com/talks/robert_waldinger_what_makes_a_good_life_lessons_from_the_longest_study_on_happiness?utm_campaign=tedspread&utm_medium=referral&utm_source=tedcomshare

If I could share one more piece of advice with my 16-year-old self, it would be this: Investing early and often is essential. I would explain the power of compound growth. Then, I would relate the historical results of investing in large US stocks, as measured by Standard and Poor's 500 (S&P 500), to illustrate the actual cost of choosing current spending over investing. The S&P 500 measures the performance of the 500 largest companies in the United States.

This book examines the historical returns of stocks and bonds. I used two sources of data for examining historical results. One was provided by Dr. Aswath Damodaran, a professor of finance at the Stern School of Business at New York University. Below, I use his data from 1928 through 2023 for the total returns on the S&P 500. Since the S&P 500 did not exist until 1957, earlier data uses other indices to measure the performance of large US companies.[2]

If a 16-year-old today decided to invest $100 in an index tracking the performance of the S&P 500 and then checked the value of this investment 49 years later at age 65, what might the results look like? No one can know how the market will perform in the future, but we can examine the range of historical results for 49-year periods starting with the one running from January 1, 1928 through December 31, 1976. Before doing that, let me state two assumptions I made in calculations. First, I assume the 16-year-old has earned at least $100 from a part-time job and contributed this money to a Roth individual retirement account (IRA), which can experience the wonders of tax-free compound growth up to the account holder turning 65. The second assumption deals with the investment's cost or expense ratio. We cannot invest directly in the S&P 500 but can invest in an index that closely tracks its performance. Mutual and exchange-traded funds (ETFs) tracking the S&P 500 can easily be found with expense ratios under 0.05%. I conservatively assume an expense ratio of 0.05% for my calculations.

What would be the result for the first 49-year sequence in 1928? If 16-year-old kids invested $100 today and experienced the market returns of 1928 through 1976, in 49 years, they would have just over $5,000, or 50 times their original investment. Sounds pretty good. In fairness, we should consider that $100 in January 1928 could purchase much more than $100 in January 1977. Reducing the result for inflation over that period still results in about $1,500. The graph below shows the result for each of the 48 sequences.

Real Value of a One-Time Investment of $100 in Stocks Over 49 Years By Start Year

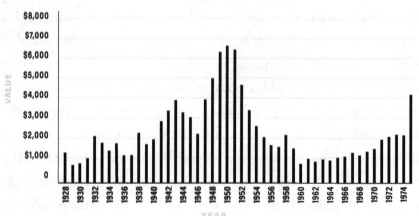

One takeaway is the large range of historical outcomes. The results show the worst 49-year span for this investment would be the one starting in 1929, yielding a little less than $900 after discounting for

49 years of inflation. The largest result, beginning in 1950, is over $6,600! The median result of all 48 sequences is about $2,000.

While the variability of the results is noteworthy, I believe there is a more important point here. Over long investment periods, the performance of stocks has consistently outpaced inflation so much so that, historically, one would have ended up with many times their original investment even after adjusting for inflation.

Does this suggest that all teenagers should become penny pinchers and deprive themselves of the pleasure of discretionary spending? No. Not all discretionary spending is the same. We value and desire some things worthy of our hard-earned money. Other things are purchased and our decision is regretted in short order. Being more intentional and less impulsive with these purchases may be a wise course of action.

If I had told my 16-year-old self all this, I would have been more selective with my spending and my retirement account would be more significant today. My 16th birthday was in late 1983. As of this writing, the S&P 500 has over 25 times its value of 1984. I would have been willing to risk losing money in the market; I had not yet taken six courses in statistics as an undergraduate nor taught college courses in statistics. The statistical argument for investing at that age still would have been persuasive. (Your mileage might vary.)

In Chapter 5, we examine a similar example, demonstrating the historical outcomes of a teenager fully funding a Roth IRA for three years. If you have a loved one around this age, consider sharing this information with them. Their future self might give you a great big thank you!

Historical data has its limitations. The future is unlikely to be a carbon copy of the past. In addition, it provides no guarantee of future performance; it may be worse than past performance and investors need to understand this. Historical data can help make rational decisions about an uncertain future, but there are no guarantees in life and investing is not exempt from this truth!

Many only seriously think about retirement planning once they are near retirement. If you plan with intention, you will prioritize it much earlier than that. Decisions made early in life can affect your situation as you approach retirement age. For this reason, an intentional retirement planning process is ongoing. Along the way, we will experience life changes that may be unexpected, perhaps even drastic. But considering our future early in life with intention will give us the best chance to adapt to any changes we may face.

So, where should retirement planning start? If you recall the subtitle of this book, "Being Intentional with Heart, Mind, and Money at Any Age," you might guess the heart. You would be correct. Heart, mind, and money were stated in that order for a reason. Money has no intrinsic value. Its value comes from what you can do with it. Knowing your best use of this finite resource involves using your mind to get in touch with your heart. Your heart contains your values, goals, desires, and sense of purpose.

The mind is a beautiful thing. It can help us discern matters of the heart. It can also absorb financial education to aid us in making reasoned decisions in the face of uncertainty. However, the mind is not flawless. Cognitive blind spots and biases can lead to poor decisions involving the heart and money. Emotions such as fear, envy, and greed can also send us down the wrong path. Chapters 1 through 3 discuss the heart, mind, and techniques to overcome cognitive deficiencies.

The ability to manage risk is an essential skill to develop. While managing your financial assets to limit exposure to risk and understanding your risk tolerance is an imperative skill I discuss in this book, risk management should extend further. What about the risk of inadequate retirement savings? Conversely, can you save too much? Yes, you can. Some super savers forgo experiences in their youth and have more money than they need in retirement. We must balance current spending choices with having more financial resources later in life. This may be the most significant challenge people face in retirement planning.

How does one act with intention when performing this balancing act? I believe many people in their 20s and 30s need to think more about their financial readiness for their 60s and beyond. Some believe there is plenty of time to save for retirement later and feel like they are light years away from even contemplating retirement. Many save little or nothing for retirement. Intentional decision-making would consider some of their current spending and how much easier it might be to save for retirement if they started investing earlier. Understanding the power of compound growth and some financial education can shed light on the costs of today's spending. Grasping the actual costs of today's discretionary spending is one of the most essential skills to learn when managing money.

Discretionary spending includes what a financial advisor charges you for their services. Many are unaware of the long-term costs for advisor fees so this book also covers the impact of such fees.

Chapters 4 through 6 introduce some essential issues about money management and investing. The best place to start is by 1) understanding where your money is going and 2) creating a yardstick to measure your financial health. Creating and monitoring a budget and tracking your net worth help achieve these two objectives. Before investing, we must consider the concept of risk and how to measure our risk tolerance. This book also discusses some common misunderstandings regarding investing.

Chapters 7 through 11 cover planning in three different life stages: pre-retirement, post-retirement, and the transitional period between them. Another aspect of the balancing act is how to measure the size of your nest egg required to meet your financial goals in retirement. The last section wraps things up with creating a written plan, a brief introduction to estate planning, and deciding on professional advice.

Retirement planning feels overwhelming for many, which is understandable because it can be complex but *Holistic Retirement Planning* discusses many of these complexities. For example, people typically focus on how to invest over a lifetime. Indeed, that is an important issue and we discuss it in this book, but there is more to consider financially. How do you get the most out of the retirement assets you end up with? If you live in the United States and qualify to receive Social Security benefits, you can choose to claim your benefit anywhere from age 62 to 70. How do you make that choice? Investments in different types of accounts are subject to different tax rates. How do you optimally draw from your nest egg in retirement? Do Social Security benefits impact the optimal withdrawal strategy? If so, how? Budgeting for health care after retirement is another hurdle to maneuver but this book addresses all the issues above.

Some individuals reading this lack any interest in managing their nest egg themselves. If you're part of that group, you may question the relevance of this information. Should you hand your nest egg to a financial advisor and let them handle it? Perhaps. But how would you know whether you hired an advisor best suited for your needs? Do you understand what services various financial advisors offer? How are they different? Are you aware that some offer fewer services but charge more? Do you understand the impact of higher fees on the size of your nest egg? You will gain some understanding of the issues within these pages.

This book caters to a broader audience than just DIY investors; it is also for those who want to hire a financial advisor since it's vital to understand the services available and their potential value. Along with this, knowledge of the impact of fees on your nest egg should make you a well-informed consumer of financial services.

I hope you enjoy reading *Holistic Retirement Planning*. My purpose in life is to use any knowledge and talents I possess to better the lives of others. From this book, I hope you gain knowledge and causes for reflection.

CHAPTER 1

—

Knowing What You Want: A Personal Game Plan

THE JOURNEY TO retirement starts by examining what you want. Money has no intrinsic value in itself, it is just a resource that can help you achieve your goals. Personal goals and lifestyle differ, so knowing what you want is essential to understanding how much money you need to reach your retirement goals.

This seems logical to me now, but I messed up this first step. How did this happen? Part of the explanation lies in how my brain is wired: I am a numbers guy who loves spreadsheets. I enjoyed studying and learning about the financial part of the journey. I focused on the numbers too much at the expense of self-reflection.

We all process information differently. Understanding yourself includes learning how you process information. Our process might be subject to cognitive blind spots or behavioral biases that can lead to poor life and financial decisions. This chapter discusses mental blind spots and offers an approach to mitigate them. Chapter 2 discusses behavioral biases.

I share some personal details of my life in this book for several reasons. Life experiences shape our views. Hopefully, you will better understand my perspective on topics covered in this book because of their inclusion. These details may also stimulate your own self-reflection and provide deeper self-awareness.

Five significant events shaped my journey in life. Two events happened within months of each other when was in my early 20s. The other three more recent events motivated me to write this book. The first event left a profound impact on me.

Someone I barely knew asked me a question roughly two months before I completed my bachelor's degree at the University of Wisconsin–Milwaukee. I had enrolled in an advanced class in the economics department. Most attendees of this class were graduate students. The professor asked me if I had thought about graduate school. The answer was no. I didn't know anyone who had gone to graduate school and thought only wealthy people could attend. In retrospect, it was a silly thought, but that's what I believed. If this professor had not asked me that question, I doubt my cognitive blind spot would have been exposed before taking a different path.

I applied for PhD programs in economics. My professor had graduated from the University of Illinois earlier that year and had left a positive impression on me, so that was where I applied and attended.

Less than two years after I completed my PhD, I accepted a job offer to work as a forensic economist. The person in charge of the job search for my position attained one of his degrees from the University of Illinois. I'm sure he had no preference for Illinois graduates. I've worked with this firm for over 25 years.

I have thought about this chain of events many times since. The profound impact of that simple question is astonishing; it changed the jobs, locations, and people who came into my life. This experience heightened my awareness of blind spots and behavioral biases and I am thankful for the lesson it taught me. I am sure I still have cognitive blind spots and behavioral biases; we all do. Awareness is the first step in addressing them. Attempts at mitigation to limit their influence on your life is the next step.

I'm sure you can relate to one of the other significant events in my life. In March 2020, everything changed in the blink of an eye. Before that, an unexpected divorce in 2019 upended my life. It was not just the divorce itself, it was also the speed at which things progressed. The ink on the divorce decree dried less than 10 weeks after I first learned I was heading for a divorce. I felt unprepared for this and the pandemic that quickly followed. I devoted many hours during lockdown to reflect on my life and plan my future. The plan below is what I came up with.

Steps to Develop My Plan

Below is the five-step process I used to create my game plan. It's not the only method, but it might work for you, too.

Step 1: Note Activities of Interest— Past, Present, and Future

You shouldn't be surprised by this. I used a spreadsheet to organize my thoughts. I reflected on things to do, creating columns in my spreadsheet for the past, present, and future. Unique times called for extraordinary measures. This special COVID edition of the spreadsheet included an additional column labeled "Right Now!" Each row contained an activity I enjoyed in the past, at present, or was considering in the future. I added each activity to all applicable columns. It took many days of self-reflection to complete a decent first draft.

Step 2: Uncover Blind Spots With Lists

Cognitive blind spots can be exposed by reviewing lists according to the 2019 *Journal of Financial Planning* article-"Goals-Based Financial Planning: How Simple Lists Can Overcome Cognitive Blind Spots." Participants in the study wrote their top three investment goals and then reviewed a master list of 17 investment goals. After viewing this list, over 70% of the participants changed at least one of their top three investment goals and 26% of participants changed their number one financial goal! Although this study focused on investment goals, its findings apply to other areas. Lists expose the mind to new possibilities.

To expand my initial list, I tried to uncover cognitive blind spots. Reading was an activity unhampered by COVID. After some online research, I purchased a copy of *How to Retire Happy, Wild, and Free: Retirement Wisdom That You Won't Get from Your Financial Advisor* by Ernie Zelinski, confident it contained ideas worth exploring for my list. I am glad I did. Zelinksi provides over 300 examples of activities retirees might consider doing. Reviewing this extensive list, I added past, present, and future ideas to my spreadsheet.

Step 3: Sort the List Into Key Categories

I desired to have enough activities in three essential categories and sorted the rows in my spreadsheet by these category types. In March 2020, the first category on my mind was interacting with others. I knew relationships were important despite not yet having seen Dr. Waldinger's 2015 TED talk. Still, I listed activities that involved socializing with others (family, friends, social groups). The second category was physical activities that provided exercise for the body. The last category was activities to engage my mind. Yes, my list eventually included becoming a first-time author.

Step 4: Ask Yourself Why

The next step in my process was reflection. For each activity, I paused and asked *why* it was on my list. That may seem unnecessary, but it increases the likelihood that you will discover more about yourself. For example, you might list travel as something that brings you happiness. Travel might bring you enjoyment for several reasons: Perhaps you travel with family or close friends and the special memories created with them are valuable to you. Maybe you travel to places you have never been before because you enjoy learning new things. History buffs like visiting historical sites for obvious reasons. Some people love nature and traveling to places of natural beauty. We could conduct a similar exploration to determine why someone enjoys going to the beach. Is it the sound of waves, the warmth of the sun, or the nostalgic value of a childhood family activity that brings you joy? When asking why, look for reoccurring themes in your answers; you may discover a goal or value is more meaningful than you originally thought.

Step 5: Additional Reflection

Further examination of activities in the future column was also fruitful. Must they wait for the future? Could I do them sooner? At the lockdown's peak, I was interested in finding activities I could do immediately. Learning to play the guitar was something that had always intrigued me and, surely, online instruction videos could guide my way. Unfortunately, the pace of my progress caused frustration, and in 2020, additional frustration was something I wished to avoid. Trying this activity brought no regrets; the timing was just wrong for me. Someday, I will pick up the guitar again, but right now, writing this book is my main creative outlet.

You may wish to take a similar path to discover your goals. If so, limit your wants and goals to workable ones. But how? We have not discussed estimating possibilities and limitations and for now, that is okay, within reason. If you wish to retire next year and travel six months each year while staying at five-star resorts on an annual budget of $15,000, remove that travel goal from your game plan. But if you think your goal may be financially workable, keep it on your current list. Perhaps the goal you have in mind is possible but would require great sacrifice to attain. A cost-benefit analysis can help assess whether the sacrifice is worth the benefit. More on this later.

People are more likely to stick to written plans so consider recording your game plan electronically, realizing things will change. Your interests or life circumstances may cause a change in your plan. If one or more of the three Big D's (death, disability, divorce) affect you, your plans may change tremendously. All three Big D's have played a role in shaping my journey.

Having a plan is excellent, but what about follow-through? Writing out your plan can generate motivation to stick with it. Saving for retirement typically takes a long time, and if you are diligent in saving, you will be delaying gratification for some time. Reflecting on your reasons for postponing some spending to save for retirement may enhance your likelihood of staying the course.

Some people hate their jobs and their primary driving force in saving as much as possible is to quit their jobs sooner. Consider a few things if this applies to your situation. Even if a potential new job would pay less, reducing stress and discontent in your life may be well worth the loss. If the sacrifice of quitting is too high or not feasible but there are ways to make your job more tolerable, seriously consider implementing these changes. Some improvement would be better than none. Examining your goals is even more critical if you are in this situation. The saying "It's better to run toward something than away from something" is true when planning for retirement.

A second benefit of planning is being better prepared for retirement. Many retirees lack a plan or direction for their time. Social connections developed in the workplace disappear. Some people become bored in a matter of months after retiring. You don't want an identity crisis if you decide to retire or significantly reduce your weekly work hours. Start learning more about who you are outside the workforce before leaving it.

CHAPTER 2

—

Your Brain, Your Money, Your Enemy

DEALING WITH MONEY involves dealing with emotions and inherent biases—biases many are unaware of and that can lead to unhealthy financial outcomes. It is essential to understand how we view money; we don't want to become our own worst enemy. Shine a light on your relationship with money and you might save yourself from a lot of grief and a much lower net worth. This chapter considers common behavioral biases, and Chapter 3 discusses ways to mitigate their influence over your financial decisions. Before discussing them, however, I think some initial self-reflection may be fruitful.

Examine Influential Events and People in Your Life

We all have tendencies or ways of thinking that have been shaped by life experiences. Biases may develop because of these experiences, so it is vital to know ourselves and reflect on what has made us think the way we do. This can better prepare us to make good decisions.

My parents were frugal. Given their backgrounds, I would have expected nothing else. My father immigrated to the United States in his teens after World War II. He had an eighth-grade education, and the only significant asset he brought with him was family. My mother shared stories of growing up with worn-out shoes and depending on others' generosity. Like my dad, she understood the value of family and the support of loved ones.

Although Mom and Dad were frugal, they would occasionally splurge on things, but only on things they deeply valued. When I was young, I could tell they watched their expenses, were interested in their children's education, and enjoyed the annual vacation to northern Wisconsin for a family fishing trip. As I grew older, my understanding deepened. I realized my father disliked his job, and those family trips were about more than just his love of fishing and spending time with family—they were an escape that gave him a sense of peace. I also deduced one of their significant splurges was paying themselves first. Neither of my parents had a high-paying job or a pension. My father retired at 56 but lived life on his terms by keeping a watchful eye on spending and wisely investing the money he paid himself. My parents' priorities also shaped my view of them.

My older brother has greatly influenced my life and is an inspiration to me. I am proud of how he has handled adversity since becoming a paraplegic in his mid-30s. Sharing a home with him for the past few years has deepened our connection and we benefit from helping each other. It sometimes requires courage and strength to make difficult decisions. He is among the few people I turn to for advice. He has played a large role in shaping my journey.

Taking the time to examine the influences on my life has been fruitful for me. I recommend you do the same.

Top 10 Behavioral Biases

We all wish to make sound, informed financial decisions, so why do many routinely make poor ones? A problem we all have is the three pounds lodged between our ears. Irrational financial decisions occur for two main reasons. The first is faulty cognitive reasoning. How our brain processes information sometimes leads us down the wrong path. The other culprit is our emotions. Fear and greed are two common emotions that cause suboptimal decisions.

What type of behavioral biases do financial advisors find in their clients? Which biases are the most common? The BeFi Barometer, a survey of 301 financial advisors, reported the percentage of specific and significant behavioral biases advisors observed in their practice. Below are the top 10 biases listed in the 2021 publication. We will cover mitigation techniques for battling some behavioral biases in Chapter 3.

Recency Bias

Recency bias is the tendency to place more weight on recent events than they deserve. People may underestimate the likelihood of economic and financial events if they haven't happened recently and give substantial weight to recent events when thinking about what future decades might be like. Some people in their 20s pick mutual funds in their company 401K plans based on market performance over the past one, three, or five years. They may believe five years is a long time for investing, but consider: Historically, stocks have shown higher average returns than bonds over extended time frames. Have bonds ever outperformed stocks for over five years? What about 10 years? Both questions can be answered affirmatively without referencing 20th-century data. A decade is a short time for market performance.

Confirmation Bias

Do you like being right? I bet you do. Just don't let the joy of being right cloud your judgment. Confirmation bias occurs when we seek information that supports our initial views while ignoring or down-playing information that refutes them. Like recency bias, this causes certain information to be given more weight than it deserves; we give too much weight to what we *want* to hear. Processing information with confirmation bias can lead to poor financial choices and subop-timal outcomes.

Framing

Politicians frame issues. They choose to present topics in a particular way to influence your views. Likewise, financial information can be presented in different ways and marketing is an area where framing is prevalent. This includes marketing financial services.

Many financial advisors get paid based on the assets under man-agement (AUM) model. The fee for financial advisors in this model is determined by a percentage of the client's managed assets. A typical annual fee is about 1% of the value of the assets managed. A standard sales pitch used by financial advisors paid under the AUM model sounds like this: When the client makes more money, the advisor also makes more money. The implication is that the financial advisor's pocketbook will not conflict with their client's. Let me highlight three key points here. First, I highly doubt you will ever see a financial advisor with the slogan, "If you give me more money, I'll make more money." Second, if a client loses money in a particular year, the advisor does not pull out their wallet and pay up. They still collect a fee. It will just be smaller than the fee they collected the year before.

The last point I wish to make is much more subtle. While the sales pitch does not say it, the inference is that compensation under the AUM model cannot produce any potential conflicts of interest between the client and the advisor. This is false. A financial advisor paid under the AUM model may provide their client with advice on when to claim Social Security benefits. Imagine their client just turned 62 and may collect now or delay payments until age 70 and receive a more significant check. Before speaking with their advisor, the client leaned toward starting Social Security payments at 62. The advisor determines the best strategy is for their client to delay collecting Social Security benefits until age 70. Will the advisor make less money if they do what is in their client's best interest and attempt to convince them to wait until age 70 to collect their Social Security benefits? Probably. Between age 62 and 70, the client will not have Social Security to live on. If the client withdraws funds for living expenses that Social Security would have covered from the assets managed by the advisor, it will reduce the balance and the advisor will earn a smaller fee. In this example, the client does better when the advisor makes less. That slogan has a lovely ring to it! We will examine the impact of advisor fees later in this book.

Familiarity Bias

We are more comfortable with things we are familiar with. That is true in many aspects of life and it also applies to personal finance. People invest more often in companies they know. Familiarity bias is also one of several reasons many Americans who invest in stocks own little or no foreign stocks. We will discuss the pros and cons of investing in foreign stocks later.

Loss Aversion Bias

Some amount of loss aversion is natural and even healthy, but a person with a loss aversion bias avoids losses more than they seek gains. There is nothing wrong with disliking the loss of money, however, this bias can result in poor financial decisions. Someone with strong loss aversion may desire their investment portfolio to have a meager chance of losing money in any year and be willing to accept a significantly lower average rate of return for this perceived level of security. But are they getting the protection they desire? Reducing the downside volatility on your portfolio is a good thing, but if it comes at the expense of much lower expected average rates of return, that needs to be considered. Suppose the genuine fear is outliving your portfolio. In that case, such a move might make them feel safe now but increase the likelihood of running out of money later in life, especially after considering the impact of inflation.

Anchoring Bias

This bias stems from placing too much importance on an arbitrary benchmark. For example, suppose a victim of anchoring bias purchases 100 shares of stock in company XYZ. They may use the original purchase price for their shares of XYZ as an anchor. Fixation on the original purchase price may influence their view of the actual value of the investment.

Mental Accounting

Some treat money differently depending on its origin or intended use. We know this behavior as mental accounting. For example, consider someone decades away from retirement receiving a $10,000 inheritance when a grandparent dies. They may want to know how to put it toward their retirement savings. Should they invest this money differently from their existing retirement investments? Why? Because it came from a different source? Conventional wisdom typically would be to invest the funds consistent with the retirement savings plan they hopefully have already developed. One caveat should be mentioned here: if this inheritance was huge, it could alter the need to take risks and change the desired asset allocation for retirement plans in the future. When significant life changes occur, one should consider revisiting and potentially revising their retirement plan. In Chapter 12, we will discuss creating and revising an investment policy statement.

Availability Bias

We make many decisions in our day-to-day lives from readily accessible information. We may make one quick decision and move right on to the next. There can be a tendency to overlook additional relevant sources of information that take time and effort to uncover. Limiting pertinent data in the decision-making process creates an availability bias. Some choices in life are not important and availability bias can be acceptable when the stakes are low. Some decisions deserve a little more of our time. But if the decision is essential, taking the time to gather comprehensive information is imperative. Making important decisions without all the information can lead to poor choices.

Inertia/Status Quo

One behavioral issue to watch out for is being too detached from monitoring your investment portfolio. A traditional portfolio of stocks and bonds aims to have an appropriate mix of assets to balance risk and reward. After a long period of solid stock performance, an unattended portfolio may drift toward an asset allocation with a more significant percentage of stocks than desired. As a result, the portfolio would be subject to more risk should there be a massive drop in the stock market. The level of risk we are willing to take with our investments also typically changes as we age. A person in their 60s will usually be more risk averse than someone in their 20s. An asset allocation should consider a risk tolerance that may change.

One word of caution here. Looking at your portfolio balance *too* often may cause fear or anxiety, especially when stock prices drop. Anxiety can lead to impulsive decisions which may not be in one's best interest. Some measures to help mitigate this behavior are discussed in the next chapter.

Endowment Effect

The endowment effect occurs when ownership of an asset causes a person to place a higher value on it. This could happen for several reasons. A person may inherit stock in a company from their uncle and, for sentimental reasons, refuse to part with it. They value the asset more than just the price of it. Conversely, a person may have purchased a stock that was a loser. Rather than admit they made a lousy investment decision, they convince themselves that the stock is worth more than its current price.

This is just an overview. Please reflect on the 10 biases presented in this chapter. Do you believe you have been the victim of them? Have any life experiences been a contributing factor? We cannot eliminate behavioral biases from our lives, but we can limit their impact. That is the subject of the next chapter.

CHAPTER 3

—

Mitigating Behavioral Biases

DETERMINING WAYS TO combat behavioral bias starts with financial education. Before investing in stocks and bonds, examine historical data by reading publications from reputable sources. We can also find historical rates of return for stocks and bonds online at sites like Yahoo Finance. I present some historical findings on stocks and bonds using data from Dr. Aswath Damodaran, a professor of finance at the Stern School of Business at New York University. One can also learn from online calculators; there are many free resources on the internet. The calculator I use in this book is FIRECalc.[3] FIRECalc

3   FIRECalc: A different kind of retirement calculator. https://www.firecalc.com/

was the first free online calculator I discovered years ago. It remains an excellent resource with many useful features, including historical data on stocks and bonds dating back to 1871. While the future won't be a replica of the past, I believe we can gain valuable insights from examining such data.

Historical data can expose behavioral biases. Below are several ways we can use this data as a tool to mitigate such biases. Then we will explore additional strategies that can help.

Financial Education

Let's examine how financial education can overcome some behavioral biases covered in Chapter 2. We begin with the most prominent behavior bias of them all: recency bias.

Recency Bias

Let's travel back in time together. The year is 2006. According to data from the US Bureau of Labor Statistics, the United States had not experienced unemployment over 8% or an annual inflation rate of over 6% in more than two decades. Because of recency bias, many believed high unemployment and inflation were a thing of the past and unlikely to occur in the next 20 years. However, unemployment in the United States was above 8% for 43 consecutive months, from February 2009 through August 2012, and an additional five months in 2020. The annual rate of inflation in the United States in 2022 was 8%.

Recency bias does not only impact people's perception of the economy's future, it also impacts their perception of how their investments will perform. Stocks have provided a higher rate of return than bonds, on average, over very long periods. This is because stocks are riskier than bonds, so a premium is paid for taking this risk. However, that does not mean there aren't times of considerable duration when bonds outperform stocks.

A review of Dr. Damodaran's data shows that the returns for the S&P 500 were very impressive from 1982 through 1999. In only one of those years, 1990, was there a loss in the S&P 500, and that loss was small—only about 3%. What about the returns in 1995 through 1999? Each of those years produced a return for the S&P 500 of over 20%! Let the good times roll! The performance of stocks trounced bonds in the 1990s. Why would the future be any different?

As you might know, the story changed in 2000. Suppose you had invested the same amount of money on January 1, 2000, in the mutual fund VBMFX (Vanguard Total Bond Market) and the mutual fund VTSMX (Vanguard Total Stock Market). If you checked your balances 15 years later, you would have found that the bond fund outperformed the stock fund. This result was fueled by the significant losses for stocks from 2000 through 2002, in 2008, and the strong performance of bonds in those same years.

The main point is this: In many aspects of life, 10 years can seem exceptionally long, but for economic and financial outcomes, 10 years is arguably a short time.

Loss Aversion

Some older adults are terrified of stocks; the volatility of stock prices creates anxiety. Many seek the safest stock/bond portfolio and believe having few to no stocks is the way to maximize safety. Their opinions may change if they review historical stock and bond performance data of Vanguard's Model Portfolio Allocation.[4] Over 96 years, from 1926 through 2021, a portfolio with 100% bonds produced an average annual return of 6.3%, losing money 20 of the 96 years, with the worst loss at 8.1%. What happens if we add a small percentage of stocks into the mix? During the same 96-year period, a portfolio with 20% stocks and 80% bonds produced an average annual rate of return of 7.5%, an increase of 1.2% per year. The years with a loss decreased from 20 to 16. The worst year of performance sees a slight uptick, with the loss increasing from 8.1% to 10.1%. However, overall, the 20% stock portfolio may be considered safer. Running out of money is a genuine fear for many older adults, and one can run out of money due to negative stock market returns or if the average rate of return is too low. Compared to a 100% bond portfolio, a long-term investment in the 20% stock portfolio may lower the likelihood of running out of money.

Does this mean a portfolio should always have stocks in it for diversification? No. First, nothing in this book is personal advice or should be taken as such. Second, this book is about retirement planning. Retirement planning is often flexible and everyone's situation is different. If your nest egg is smaller than desired as you approach a targeted retirement age, delaying retirement or starting a side hustle may be an option. Some may be able to revise their budget after experiencing unanticipated financial situations. In retirement, some may work part-time if they retain the necessary physical and cognitive abilities. In short, some options allow for plan flexibility.

Consider a short-term investment for a down payment on a home. Someone in this situation may decide to invest all their money in

4   https://investor.vanguard.com/investor-resources-education/education/model-portfolio-allocation

a certificate of deposit (CD) because they want the chance of losing money to be zero. The reason for investment and your risk tolerance can guide how you invest.

Familiarity Bias

Some purchase company stocks because they love the products they make. For example, consider Apple. Many people love iPhones and are devoted fans of Macintosh computers. Apple might be a fine stock to invest in, but a person using this logic to handpick stocks should realize that the price of a stock reflects future expectations for the company based on all known information. Are they the first person on the planet to think Apple makes beautiful products and is likely to produce beautiful products in the future? To the extent such information applies to the price of a stock, it is already baked into the cake. Many remarkable companies elude our awareness. Should we only invest in the companies we know? Diversification can be an effective way to reduce risk in an investment portfolio. Reducing your investments to only companies you are confining with reduces diversification and can increase investment risk.

Availability Bias

The more you learn about personal finance, the more aware you become of your knowledge gaps. Concepts or tools you were oblivious to may become things you know little about, but at least you realize their existence. Information on many topics and financial tools is just a web search away—once you know what to look up. For example, you may be familiar with the phrase "sequence of return risk." Monte Carlo simulations are another powerful tool used by do-it-yourself investors and financial advisors.

Set Up Rules and Procedures to Address Behavioral Biases

One of the best ways to set SMART (specific, measurable, achievable/actionable, relevant/realistic, time-bound) goals is with an investment policy statement.

Develop an Investment Policy Statement

An investment policy statement (IPS) is a written document stating investment goals and strategies. For example, Julie may aim to reach $1 million in her stock and bond portfolio by age 62. The goal is *specific*. She can *measure* progress toward this goal. The IPS will also state the *actions* needed to attain this goal. For example, after performing statistical analysis, Julie might believe she can *realistically* achieve her goal if she saves and invests 20% of her annual gross pay. Also, Julie's IPS would state her asset allocation. For example, say she decides on the proper asset allocation based on her ability, willingness, and need to take risks. This portfolio includes 60% stocks (75% domestic, 25% foreign) and 40% US bonds. Managing her portfolio would consist of other details and cover how she would monitor and act based on rules set up to avoid behavioral bias. And of course, there is also a *time* frame to reach the goal. This is just an introduction to an IPS and its general purpose. Chapter 12 is devoted to creating an IPS.

Using autopilot

In the example above, Julie contributes 20% of her gross pay toward her portfolio. If she makes this contribution in a company retirement plan, like a 401(k), she could automate her contribution. If she does not automate her contributions, it may tempt her to time them based on current market conditions. As discussed in the next chapter, most people lose money when attempting to time the market.

In Chapter 2, we discussed inertia. It is best to rebalance a portfolio to the asset allocation stated in your IPS to avoid exposing yourself to more risk than desired, which might occur after a period of strong performance of stocks relative to bonds. Workplace retirement accounts like 401(k)s usually offer periodic rebalancing to return the portfolio to its intended asset allocation. Some people pick a specific date to rebalance, such as their birthday. Others use a rule allowing the asset allocation to drift within an acceptable range. For example, consider a person who has chosen a simple two-fund portfolio, 60% total US stock market and 40% total US bond market. An IPS might state that rebalancing should occur if stocks fall outside a range of 55% to 65%. To avoid behavioral bias, rebalancing should follow a rule in your IPS and not be driven by impulsive thoughts or fear.

Taxes should also be a consideration when rebalancing a portfolio. Rebalancing tax-advantaged accounts like a 401(k) or IRA never creates tax liability but it can create one in a brokerage account. However, you can rebalance your brokerage account portfolio without touching it. Your overall asset allocation across all investment accounts is what really matters. Adjusting investments in tax-advantaged accounts can return a portfolio to the desired asset allocation. What if it is not possible? If you wish to avoid taxes and are saving for retirement, you can use new contributions to nudge your portfolio to its intended asset allocation. You may do something similar in retirement by withdrawing more from an overweight asset class. When taxes are involved, weighing the advantages of rebalancing your allocation against the associated tax expenses is prudent.

Reduce News Intake

It is nice to be informed, however, watching or reading the news can also create anxiety or activate recency bias. As with many things, you need to find the proper balance. Just be aware of the potential problem created by being "too informed."

Getting Information from Diverse Sources

Getting financial information from different reliable sources can provide us with different perspectives. This is one way to combat availability bias. It also helps fight against framing. Making the right decision is often dependent upon remaining open to new information.

Take Time to Reflect

Just as it is wise to reflect on your personal game plan, the same is true for your financial plan. I strongly encourage devoting significant time to reflection when creating an IPS, but reflection should not end there. New situations or information will present themselves and some could tempt a knee-jerk response to act. Taking your time allows for better decision-making. Impulsive decisions can produce costly outcomes.

Don't Peek Too Much

It is a good idea to monitor your investments, and an IPS typically states how you will do this. There is no single correct frequency for monitoring your progress. Some review their progress upon receiving a quarterly statement. Others feel more comfortable with a monthly schedule. Regardless, if reviewing account balances tempts you to override your IPS and do something impulsive, consider examining them less often.

CHAPTER 4

—

Tracking Net Worth and Creating a Budget

THIS BOOK STARTED with a five-step process to understand our life goals and used lists to expose cognitive blind spots. Making decisions can be challenging, especially when our minds get in the way. Behavioral biases are another obstacle that influences how our brain processes the information it receives. After clarifying our goals and achieving an awareness of behavioral biases and approaches to dealing with them, it's time to move on to financial decisions on the holistic journey to retirement. Where do we start? Understanding our current financial situation.

Statement of Financial Position

There are two key financial statements in personal finance. One of them is called a statement of financial position or a personal financial statement. These terms describe a document or spreadsheet that outlines an individual's assets and liabilities as of a specific date.

Let's begin our discussion by listing assets on a financial position statement. Some assets have distinct qualities and you may wish to categorize them. If you need money urgently, the value of your home would take time to be beneficial—it is not a "liquid" asset. Liquid balances in checking or savings accounts are helpful during emergencies. Considering these factors, assets can be categorized into three groups.

1. **Cash and cash equivalents**—Balances in savings accounts, checking accounts, and short-term CDs are highly liquid. We can access them quickly with minimal penalties, if any.
2. **Invested assets**—This would include balances in IRAs, workplace retirement accounts such as 401(k) plans, and brokerage accounts.
3. **Use assets**—Possessions that could be sold at their current fair market value might include the present value of real estate, vehicles, and collectibles. Typically, we only include assets of significant value.

After listing all the assets, add up their total value. Then, move on to liabilities.

Liabilities are often listed in order from short-term to long-term obligations. Liabilities appearing on a statement of financial position might include a current credit card balance or the principal owed on a home, car, or student loan.

Net worth is the total value of assets minus the total value of liabilities. Net worth can be positive or negative. For example, many recent college graduates start with a negative net worth because they have few assets of value but a significant student loan debt to pay off.

I want to make a final point about emergencies before moving on: Many people in the United States need to increase the amount of money they have in a checking or savings account to cover emergency expenses. One option may be to withdraw money from an IRA or an employer-sponsored retirement plan, but taxes and early withdrawal penalties may make this option undesirable. There are some exceptions to the early withdrawal penalty depending on the type of account you are withdrawing from and the reason for the withdrawal. For example, both IRAs and employer-sponsored plans have exceptions for death, disability, and medical costs over 7.5% of income and allow withdrawals of up to $5,000 per parent for birth or adoption. IRAs offer some additional exceptions, including educational expenses, up to $10,000 toward the purchase of a home for a first-time home buyer, and the cost of health insurance while unemployed. Investigate these exceptions before withdrawing from any retirement account, as they are subject to change. Selling stocks or bonds in a brokerage account is another option as it never involves paying a withdrawal penalty, but there may be tax consequences.

Net Worth in the United States

If you live in the United States, you might wish to compare your net worth to your fellow Americans. One resource is an October 2023 publication by the Board of Governors of the Federal Reserve System entitled "Changes in US Family Finances from 2019 to 2022: Evidence from the Survey of Consumer Finances".[5] A section of this publication provides average and median net worth figures by income, age, education, and race or ethnicity. The most recent estimates in this publication report that the median family net worth is $192,900, and the average net worth is $1,063,700. However, this average is a pretty useless statistic when measuring net worth; households in the top 1% have a net worth of over $13 million, which skews the average. The median better represents "typical" values.

While the publication provides an excellent overview, we can find additional insights using the free online calculator Net Worth by Age Percentile Calculator–United States.[6] It utilizes the same raw data as the publication I mentioned above but allows a more granular examination of the data. Select an age bracket and type in a net worth figure. When you hit calculate, it will display the percentile for that net worth and produce a graph showing the net worth for each percentile from the 10th percentile to the 99th. For example, suppose you are 52 years old, computed your net worth as $525,000, and wish to know how that compares to other people your age. You would place in the 64th percentile of US net worth for ages 50 to 54 in 2023; you are doing better than 64% of the American population as the median net worth for that age bracket is $266,140—just over half of what you have. About 20% have a net worth below $30,142. How are the

5   scf23.pdf (federalreserve.gov)

6   dqydj.com

top 2% in your age bracket doing? They have a net worth of at least $8.5 million.

A critical note on net worth: While it may be interesting to see where you stand relative to others, it is essential to remember that money is just a tool to achieve your goals. Spending too much time comparing yourself to others is unhealthy. Your ultimate target for net worth will depend on your personal game plan. If the things in life you value and give you the most pleasure and satisfaction are free or inexpensive, you may live a much wealthier life than someone with double or triple your financial net worth.

Human and Investment Capital

It is important to consider two main types of capital: human capital and investment capital. Human capital is a person's skills or abilities that allow them to sell their labor in the workforce. College students pursuing a degree typically are trying to enhance their human capital. Young people generally have a high value of human capital as they have many years of working life ahead of them. As a person ages, their total lifetime value of human capital diminishes or is eliminated. After retirement, Social Security and investment capital assets play a prominent role.

Investment capital, the value of a person's investments, often starts low or is nonexistent. A consistent pattern of diversified long-term investing is a proven formula to build investment capital, a key component of many people's net worth. Earnings generated from human capital pay current expenses and can also be used to pay yourself. You must make many decisions if you are earning an income. *Should I pay myself a portion of this money and invest it? If I do, what percentage of my paycheck should I devote to investment? How should I invest this money? Would this percentage be sufficient to meet my financial goals?* Answering these essential questions can be challenging as the market's performance is unpredictable. In hindsight, you may have saved more or less than needed to meet your financial goals but it's better to have reasonable savings estimates than none.

Flexibility may be required to adjust for unexpected changes in your financial position. If a shortfall is expected, consider starting a side hustle to earn more money, delaying retirement, working a part-time job after retirement, cutting current expenses, or lowering your acceptable standard of living in retirement.

The above discussion provides a general overview of common retirement planning challenges associated with building net worth. The tradeoff between current consumption and investing to provide for future consumption is difficult for most people. Understanding this tradeoff is best achieved through a series of steps. The first step is creating a budget.

Cash Flow Statement

Another key financial statement in personal finance is a cash flow statement. It documents the inflow and outflow of money over a specified period and is one way to establish a budget. Inflows include items such as gross salaries, dividend income from a stock portfolio, capital gains from an investment portfolio, interest income, and other sources of income such as alimony, pension benefits, and Social Security benefits. All these sources are added together to arrive at a total inflow.

Total outflows can be calculated by combining three categories: needs, wants, and savings/debt payment. Must-haves such as housing, utilities, basic food, essential clothing, the minimum required payment on a credit card bill, and medical care are all examples of outflow needs. We *want* vacations, streaming subscriptions, to dine out, and buy designer clothing or concert tickets. Examples of items categorized as savings/debt payment may include debt payments beyond the minimum required, contributions to an emergency fund, savings for a down payment on a home, and contributions to retirement accounts. There is a net deficit if total inflows are less than total outflows. A net surplus exists if the converse is true. If total outflows equal total inflows, there is a zero net surplus. One method of budgeting is called zero-based budgeting and its goal is a zero net surplus each month.

Keeping tabs on income and expenses over time offers insight into money movement. Suppose someone feels they need to cut back on expenses. What process might they use to reach this goal? One approach is to start with an examination of the wants. Identify the expenses that provided you with the slightest pleasure and consider eliminating them. Are your subscriptions underutilized? Realize that cutting down on an expense category does not necessarily mean eliminating it or reducing the frequency of its occurrence. For example, if you spend a lot on dining out, you could dine out less often to lower that expense. But choosing to dine out at less expensive restaurants or being more selective at selecting items on the menu at your favorite regular spots could accomplish the same goal. Would these options for cost reduction have a measurable impact on your enjoyment of dining out? The same type of exercise could apply to a vacation budget.

What is the ideal percentage distribution for the three general outflow types? One popular suggestion is 50% to needs, 30% to wants, and the remaining 20% to savings/debt payment. The origins of this 50/30/20 budget rule have been attributed to the book written by Sen. Elizabeth Warren and her daughter Amelia Warren Tyagi, *All Your Worth: The Ultimate Lifetime Money Plan.* While this advice may work well for some, it may not be suitable for others for various reasons. First, people's living costs differ based on location. A person living in San Francisco, California, should expect to allocate a much more significant percentage of their outflows to necessities such as housing than someone living in Tulsa, Oklahoma.

If you want to retire early, a higher saving rate may be required. People in the Financial Independence Retire Early (FIRE) movement generally have very high savings rates, often up to or over 50%. This increased savings level can help some individuals achieve financial freedom in their 30s, 40s, or 50s but the percentage you need to save depends on the retirement lifestyle you envision. The higher your expenses, the greater your savings requirements.

Suppose we are considering saving, say, an extra 5% of our total inflows for retirement investing by reducing spending by 5%. How can we determine the benefits of delaying gratification? We cannot know the answer since the future performance of our investments is unknown, but studying historical investment returns helps us gain insight into potential outcomes. I discuss this type of information in Chapter 6. When you save money, you forgo current spending. The more you understand the costs and benefits of saving, the better saving decisions you are likely to make.

Average Spending in the United States

Are you curious about how the average American household spends its money? The US Bureau of Labor Statistics conducts the Consumer Expenditure Survey and reports this data type. The figures below come from Table 1502 of the 2021 CES, published in September 2022. In 2021, there were about 133,595,000 households in the United States, with an average of 2.4 people per household. Their average income before taxes was $87,432, with an average after-tax income of $78,743. Here are some of the significant annual expenditures reported: $22,624 for housing, $8,229 for food ($5,259 for food at home and $3,030 for food away from home), $4,223 for utilities, $10,961 for transportation (including $2,148 for gasoline, other fuels, and motor oil), $5,452 for health care, and $3,568 for entertainment.

Budgeting Methods

We have already discussed zero-based budgeting and the 50/30/20 budget. There is nothing magical about the specific 50/30/20 percentages representing needs, wants, and savings/debt reduction; needs and savings/debt reduction differ based on personal circumstances. For example, a person living in an area with a high cost of living may use 60% of their income for needs and develop a 60/20/20 budget plan, while a person prioritizing early retirement may have a 50/20/30 budget.

Two other approaches deserve mention. The first is the envelope system. This is like zero-based budgeting, except all transactions are in cash. Cash is placed in envelopes for all the outflow categories you wish to track based on your values and needs. If you run out of money in an envelope, you either stop spending on that category or take money from a different envelope. Suppose you have several envelopes representing wants and borrow multiple times from a specific envelope. In that case, you may gain an awareness of the relative importance within your group of wants and make adjustments to your budget.

Another approach is a pay-yourself-first budget. A particular amount or percentage of income is dedicated to paying off debt or adding to savings. After that, you can spend the remaining inflows any way you wish. Those who focus on paying off high-interest debt and saving for retirement without spending much time considering expenses often find this approach desirable. There is one drawback to this budgeting method: Of the four methods discussed, it is the least likely to result in optimal spending in line with one's values.

Net Worth and Budgeting Tools

There are many budgeting tools and apps for your laptop, tablet, or phone and some also track net worth. As with any other opinions expressed in this book, none should be taken as personal advice. We are all different and a particular budgeting style could be more suitable and effective for you than for me. Also, depending on your needs, some tools may be a better fit to help you attain your goals. With that in mind, below are four good options currently available. One is free, and three require paid subscriptions.

Empower (Formerly Known As Personal Capital)

Empower is free and allows users to link investment accounts, bank accounts, and credit cards. With Empower, you can track net worth and work on budgeting. However, the budgeting tools with Empower are rather basic. To take a deeper dive into budgeting, you might consider other alternatives.

What makes Empower a very attractive option are its features outside of budgeting. The net worth tracker is handy. Even some paid budgeting apps, including one of those mentioned below, do not include the ability to track net worth. The fact that it is included in a free app is a welcome touch. Its impressive free wealth management tools are the icing on the cake and what makes Empower shine. You can track the asset allocation of all your investments, which may be in several accounts. It also has a retirement planner and a retirement fee analyzer. This provides an estimated impact of investment fees, including advisor fees, over the rest of your investment time horizon. This can be a real eye-opener!

Whenever a for-profit business offers something for free, I ask myself *What is in it for them? How are they making any money from their free offer?* Mint joined the dinosaurs on the extinction list in 2024. It was a free and popular budgeting app and made its money through ad revenue. Empower monetizes its free offering differently; it offers an upsell. They can manage your assets for a fee. If you use Empower and have a sizable net worth, don't be surprised if they pitch their wealth management services to you.

I consider Empower a Swiss army knife for financial planning. For a free app, it has an impressive list of features that goes beyond what I've mentioned. However, the budgeting tools in Empower may leave one desiring something more. One option would be to use Empower for tracking net worth and managing wealth while turning to an alternative for budgeting. Below are three budgeting alternatives you may wish to consider.

Tiller Money

Tiller Money might be your preferred budgeting tool if you love spreadsheets and highly value the ability to customize the examination of your finances. Tiller Money allows you to connect bank accounts, credit cards, mortgages, and investment accounts with Google Sheets or Microsoft Excel. The information is automatically updated every day and Tiller can email you daily with a list of new transactions and your current account balances. Placing all your transactions into the appropriate categories is easier with the ability to create auto-categorization rules, but it still requires some work.

Tiller Money has a foundation template with sheets to track expenses, set budgets, and figure net worth. Tiller Community members have also created many free templates that allow users much customization. Do you want to track information for your small business? Do you want to investigate how soon your mortgage will be paid off if you increase your monthly payment by a certain amount? There are free templates for that. Tiller also works well with a variety of budgeting methods. Currently, Tiller Money offers a free 30-day trial period, then it's $79 per year.

You Need A Budget (YNAB)

You Need a Budget (YNAB) is a popular budgeting app using zero-based budgeting. It currently has over 17,000 reviews on Google Play with an average rating of 4.6. YNAB embraces four rules, and every dollar is assigned a job according to the first three rules, which include covering infrequent expenses and surprises. This makes for a future-focused budget plan.

One unique feature, rule number four, examines the age of your money. YNAB tracks the time between new money inflow and when it is spent. This may provide insights that other tools do not and is one way to measure progress in your financial health. If your money's age increases over time, it indicates improved financial strength. If you wish to use the zero-based budgeting method and are willing to pay for a budgeting tool, YNAB is worth consideration. Unlike Tiller and Empower, YNAB does not track net worth. As of this writing, YNAB offers a free 34-day trial period and you don't even have to provide your credit card information to start the trial. They appear confident in the service's ability to attract paying customers after a trial. YNAB is more expensive than Tiller Money; it costs $99 for the annual plan or $14.99 a month.

Monarch Money

Another budgeting tool is Monarch Money. Like Tiller and Empower, you can connect your account information, track net worth, and work on budgeting. There are a few areas where Monarch Money excels. The learning curve required to use this tool is not as steep as Tiller or YNAB, and it has an excellent user interface. It is also a platform that works well for couples. You can invite your significant other or anyone you wish to collaborate with you—such as financial coaches or advisors—at no additional cost. After receiving a personal login, they can join you in exploring your finances. Just ensure you trust anyone you invite as they will have full access to your account. Currently, Monarch Money offers a 7-day free trial. After that, it costs $99.99 annually or $14.99 a month.

The Right Tool(s) for You

The right tools for you depend on their capabilities and your willingness to pay for them. Empower offers a free option that includes budgeting, net worth, and wealth management tools. You can pair Empower with any of the three mentioned apps—all offer free trials which can help you gauge whether their expense is justified in your case—or you can select a different one that best suits your needs and budget.

So far, the focus has been on budgeting and tracking net worth. What if you plan to manage your portfolio and desire good wealth management tools? Are there any additional tools to consider? Yes. Empower has the best set of free wealth management tools, but if you are willing to pay, another option is New Retirement. In my opinion, the wealth management tools of New Retirement rival the expensive software used by financial advisors and are arguably the best "low-cost" tool for do-it-yourself retirement planning. New Retirement includes net worth tracking and some impressive tools to manage your wealth. It offers a basic free version but it lacks some valuable features that Empower provides. Their lowest-cost subscription plan, PlannerPlus, costs $120 annually.

Saving More Without Saving More?

No, I'm not about to perform a magic trick and create free money out of thin air. I am talking about credit card cash-back rewards. Suppose you pay off your credit card balances in full each month and resist the temptation to increase spending. In that case, you can grow your savings without changing your spending behavior. Using this strategy is unnecessary, but how much it could add to your bottom line over a long period might surprise you.

Cash-back credit cards fall into three general categories: The first type offers a flat reward rate for all purchases. People with good credit ratings often qualify for a 1.5% or 2% cash-back credit card with no annual fee.

The second type of cash-back credit card has bonus categories. With this card type, select categories can provide anywhere from 3% to 6% cash back, while all other purchases typically give only 1% cash back.

The third type of cash-back card offers rotating categories, usually changing every three months, with 5% cash back on certain categories that quarter. These cards typically have spending caps to earn rewards. Like the bonus category cards, charges outside the premium categories typically give only a 1% cash-back reward.

Several websites provide good information on credit card offers. One of my favorites is allcards.com. The site makes recommendations based on the type of credit card and your credit score. Let's look at a method to develop your best credit card cash-back strategy.

Step 1: Check Your Credit Rating

Start with your credit rating; it will determine the credit cards you have an excellent chance of qualifying for. Allcards.com has recommendations for four different ranges of credit scores.

Step 2: Examine Your Budget

How do you choose to spend your money? If you are considering cash-back cards with bonus or rotating categories, this information will help determine which cards may give you the most value. Some common bonus categories include groceries, dining out, gasoline, travel, and streaming services. One card, the BILT Mastercard, allows you to earn points by paying rent! You will also want to note where you shop. Rotating categories may include money spent at popular stores, such as Walmart. Places like Amazon and Target also have store credit cards that offer up to 5% cash back or a discount on purchases.

Step 3: Identify Your Base Card

Find the cash-back credit card with the highest net cash back if you use only one credit card for all purchases. Start by looking at flat-rate reward cards; most have no annual fee. If your best one-card option with a flat reward rate is a 2% cash-back card with no annual fee, you have established a minimum 2% cash-back potential on your purchases. This will be the card for all your purchases unless a bonus or rotating category card can beat an effective average of 2% cash back.

Step 4: Consider Adding Additional Cards

Assume that in step 3 you ended up with a base card offering a 2% cash-back card on all purchases with no annual fee. Are there any cash-back credit cards that will net over 2% cash back with selective usage after subtracting any yearly fee? If so, does it justify your time and effort to add it to your cash-back strategy?

For example, suppose you spend an average of $150 a week in groceries to feed your two-person household and are considering the Blue Cash Preferred® Card from American Express. Currently, this card offers 6% cash back on groceries up to $6,000 annually, then only 1% after that. Additional perks include 6% cash back on streaming services and 3% cash back on gas and transit charges. They waive the $95 annual fee for the first year. There is also a $250 welcome bonus after spending $3,000 in the first six months of having the card. By selectively using this card, you could increase your total cash back compared with your base card.

For a moment, ignore the perks offered in year one. If you use this card for a second year, the additional cash back on groceries alone increases your total net cash back; the first $6,000 spent on groceries nets an extra $145 in cash back over your base card. How did I come up with $145? The difference in cash back for groceries on the first $6,000 spent would be 4% (6% minus 2%) multiplied by $6,000 or $240. After subtracting the $95 annual fee in year two, that still leaves $145. With more than a 2% cash-back rate, the second card has three other categories that could be valuable. With a waived annual fee and a $250 welcome bonus, year one would have been even better.

Research credit cards you believe add significant value to your cash-back strategy. If the added benefit of the additional card is worth the hassle of managing it, add it.

This concludes our introduction to budgeting and tracking net worth. In Chapter 5, we begin our discussion about investing.

CHAPTER 5

—

Common Misunderstandings About Investing

A FEW YEARS ago, an attorney who had hired me called with an interesting situation. His client was involved in an accident and took out a loan for $10,000 to help pay living expenses. Six years had passed since the client had taken out the loan, but he had paid none of his debt. The attorney sought information on the client's outstanding loan balance, so I asked about the interest rate for the loan. The attorney told me it was 8%. No, not 8% per year, this loan was 8% a *month!* Without calculating, what do you estimate the loan balance to be? Maybe 25 times the loan amount? Or 50 times, or even 100 times?

We can make a good approximation using the rule of 72. This rule of thumb says if you divide 72 by the rate of increase, it will tell you roughly how long it takes to double. Based on this rule of thumb, the balance on the loan would double every nine months ($72 \div 8 = 9$). It would be about $20,000 after nine months, $40,000 after 18 months, $80,000 after 27 months, and $160,000 after 36 months. After 72 months—six years—this rule of thumb would estimate a loan balance of $2,560,000! How close is this estimate to the actual answer? The estimate is only about 0.4% higher than the exact amount of $(1.08)^{72}$ times $10,000, or $2,549,825. Ironically, this difference is also about the size of the original loan.

People often underestimate the true power of compounding and this type of misunderstanding can lead to poor financial decisions. Like uncovering cognitive blind spots and exposing behavior biases, it is best to examine them before investing for retirement. Let's explore three common misunderstandings that can cause poor financial choices. The first is related to the power of compounding.

1. Underestimating the Impact of Time in the Market

As you walk into your local bank, a teller you know greets you. They present a special offer. They will give you *two* crisp, brand-new, $20 bills if you give them $20. No way! There must be a catch. They say, "No, we are just handing out free money today to our clients interested in receiving it."

Although this never occurs, something similar happens daily. Employers with a 401(k) plan often match the money contributed by their employees up to a certain percentage of their pay. Some do not contribute enough to get all the free money their employer offers. How often does this happen? Vanguard has an annual publication that answers this and many other questions about the roughly five million people participating in a Vanguard-defined contribution plan, "How America Saves 2023".[7] According to the publication, nearly 30% of individuals miss out on their employer's full free money because of insufficient contributions. This would never happen if offered cash at a bank. Why the significant difference in behavior? One reason is you could spend the bank's money right away. While that is arguably the main reason, there is another one. Most people are unaware of the actual cost of rejecting that free money. Let's examine this further.

To show the impact of time in the market, we will return to Dr. Damodaran's data source discussed in the introduction. With 96 years of data on US stock returns, from 1928 through 2023, we can examine the historical importance of time spent investing in the stock market. Consider the following example.

Jim, 25, just landed a new job with a $50,000 annual salary. His employer offers a 5% dollar-for-dollar match on a company-provided 401(k) retirement plan. Jim decides to contribute 15% of his gross salary to this plan. Including his employer match, he invests a total of $10,000 in his employer-provided 401(k) retirement plan with an index fund that tracks the S&P 500. The cost for this index fund is minimal, with an expense ratio of only 0.02%. Jim's salary is assumed to grow with the rate of inflation, and 20% of his salary will be invested this way until Jim retires at 65.

7   Access it at how-america-saves-report-2023.pdf (vanguard.com)

What can history tell us about the amount of money Jim might have in his 401(k) plan at age 65? I used Dr. Damodaran's data source to examine 40-year increments between 1928 and 2023; the earliest period would be 1928 through 1967, and the latest one spans 1984 through 2023. This gives 57 separate 40-year sequences to examine. The median outcome for Jim was $2,115,455 in today's dollars. In other words, $400,000, adjusted for inflation, was invested over 40 years. On average, the S&P 500 outpaced inflation enough that with compound growth, the median outcome of $400,000 of contributions grew to $2,115,455 over 40 years, with half of the 57 outcomes being larger and half being smaller. We can get a more conservative estimate with the 25th percentile result. Only 25% of the sequences produced an ending balance of less than $1,669,689. With the 25th percentile outcome, the investment quadrupled in size after adjusting for inflation. Even the smallest historical outcome, $1,343,816, was more than triple the real amount invested over 40 years. The 75th percentile outcome was $2,576,995, maxing over $3.6 million.

What would happen if Jim delayed investing in his 401(k) plan? After all, he's only 25 years old. There is considerable time left to save for retirement, right? The chart below performs the same analysis, assuming Jim delayed contributing to his 401(k) plan. The analysis of beginning at ages of 30, 35, and 40 removes the contributions for the first five, ten, and 15 years, respectively. Results are shown for five levels of market performance: the minimum historical outcome, the 25th percentile, the median, the 75th percentile, and the maximum historical outcome. For each level of market performance, there are four bars. The tallest bar shows the balance if investing begins at age

25. Each subsequent bar shows the ending balance at age 65, resulting from an additional five-year investment delay.

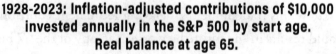

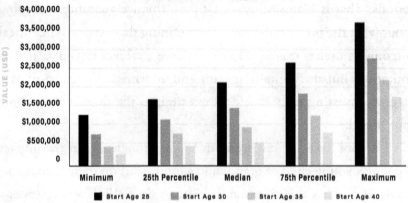

Delaying the start of retirement plan contributions from 25 to age 30 lowered the median historical outcome by about 33%, or $691,438. Over those five years, $50,000 inflation-adjusted contributions could have been added; $12,500 free money from the employer and $37,500 from Jim. If the next 40 years of investing yield results like the median outcome, Jim would sacrifice $37,500 in today's dollars over five years to gain an extra $691,438 in his retirement account at age 65. If Jim were to live on the inflation-adjusted $50,000 in retirement, it would be the equivalent of almost 14 years of retirement expenses! That is a strong incentive for Jim to contribute to his company 401(k) plan as soon as possible.

The chart above shows that delaying investment by five years would have considerably impacted the ending balance at age 65, regardless of the start year that would dictate market conditions for the next 40 years. It also suggests that if Jim waited until age 30 to contribute to his retirement but desired results like someone starting five years earlier, he would have to boost his contribution rate significantly. It would be wise to know this tradeoff before delaying retirement contributions.

Could results in the future be worse than any of the 57 historical periods? That is a possibility—past performance guarantees nothing about what the future will bring. Is examining these types of historical outcomes a useless exercise? I don't believe so. Historical data has its limitations but also contains meaningful information. Historical data suggests investing early in life allows time in the market to become your friend.

I do not have any children but I have thought about the impact of giving a young child or grandchild a jump-start on their retirement, provided one has the means and desire to do so. Below is a strategy I would consider employing, but as previously stated, readers should interpret nothing in this book as personal advice.

Imagine you have a loved one who is approaching their 16th birthday. They plan to work part-time while in high school and college and expect to earn $15,000 per year. You approach them with an offer: For three full years, from age 16 through 18, if they contribute half the maximum allowable contribution to a Roth IRA, you will give them the other half to deposit in their account. In 2024, individuals under 50 could contribute up to $7,000 to an IRA. You each would contribute $3,500 per year with any inflationary increases in the contribution limits for an IRA. As in the example above, assume 100% of this money is invested in an index fund tracking the S&P 500, this time with an expense ratio of 0.05%. Contributions are made for three years, total $21,000, and the account remains untouched until the loved one is 65.

What were the results based on the same 96 years of historical data? The period we are interested in examining is 49 years long, from age 16 through 64. The median outcome of all 49-year sequences was an inflation-adjusted amount of $394,955. The range was between $188,145 and $1,178,717; 90% of the 49-year historical sequences resulted in at least $224,968, and 95% resulted in at least $210,996—all from investing $21,000 in today's dollars. The results for the 5th percentile suggest the following after adjusting for the effects of inflation: Suppose the performance of the S&P 500 over the next 49 years is significantly below the historical average. Even in that case, the loved one might still end up with over 10 times the total amount invested and over 20 times the total amount they contributed to the Roth IRA.

When I was 16, saving for retirement was the furthest thing from my mind and I expect that is the case for most 16-year-old kids today. In my case, new technology captivated me and I spent a large portion of my earnings from my part-time job on shiny new compact discs (CDs). Some of these digital delights were enjoyable and worth the cost. Others were not. I would be much better off today if I had purchased certificates of deposit CDs rather than music CDs. It seemed hard to delay gratification for long-term goals. *I want it now, not later.* If I had been exposed in my youth to what we covered in this section, I would have altered my consumption behavior and started investing earlier. It's too late for me, but it might not be for someone else.

How much money does the typical American contribute to their 401(k) plan each year? According to the Vanguard study, the median contribution to an employer plan in 2022 was 10.6% of pay. The median employee deferral was 6.4% of income, with the remaining

4.2% from the employer. According to Vanguard, the percentage of contributions by employees increases with age and years on the job. It also increases as income rises, at least up to $150,000 in pay; because of contribution limits, many earning over $150,000 may not invest as much as desired in their employer-sponsored plans. I am convinced that increased awareness of the information in this section would lead to a higher median deferral of employees in retirement plans.

There are legitimate reasons young people save less. For one, it is harder to save a significant percentage of income when starting out. Earnings are typically much lower than others' and competing goals may exist, including paying off student loan debt and saving for a down payment on a home. If this is your situation, you may not feel you can immediately contribute as much as you would like for retirement, but contribute whatever you are comfortable with, knowing the importance of time in the market. Later, consider paying yourself a portion of any future wage increases first until reaching your targeted contribution rate. This rate would have an acceptable probability of meeting your financial planning goals. Wage increases often significantly outpace inflation during the initial three to five years of experience. Avoiding lifestyle creep by adding the raise amount exceeding inflation to retirement contributions can be a relatively painless way to significantly ramp up your contributions within five years.

2. Overestimating the Ability to Beat the Market

How well do you think you can pick individual stocks? How about that financial advisor who claims they have a secret sauce? The publication, SPIVA® (S&P Indices Versus Active) Scorecard, sheds light on this issue. It measures the relative performance of actively managed stock mutual funds and index funds targeting the same type of stocks. Published twice per year, it has existed for approximately two decades.

The most noteworthy finding is that most actively managed funds significantly underperform their benchmark over lengthy periods. Over 10 to 20 years, often less than 10% of actively managed funds beat index funds investing in similar types of companies.

The discovery of the SPIVA' Scorecard was like a mic-drop moment for me. Over 10 or more years, professional fund managers who get paid to pick the best stocks are beaten by index funds more often than I had ever imagined. Presumably, the average investor knows less about stocks than these "professionals" do. That begs this question: Why do individual stock pickers believe they can outperform index funds despite most professionals failing to do so? Maybe they have never heard of the SPIVA' Scorecard or considered its lessons. You might review the outcomes reported in it before investing in individual stocks or relying on an "expert's" advice.

3. Underestimating the Cost of Financial Advice

Most financial advisors use the assets under management (AUM) model to collect fees for their work. Below, we will examine how this compensation method might affect a client's bottom line during the accumulation phase (before retirement) and the withdrawal phase (after retirement). What do financial advisors who use this compensation model typically charge? To get a better picture, I signed up for the Bob Veres 2020 Inside Information Fee Report.[8] This 2020 survey of 1,037 advisors confirmed that most advisors used the AUM model. For clients with managed portfolios between $250,000 and $2 million, many advisors using the AUM model charge at least 1% of AUM, with 1% being the most common fee. If a client's portfolio was between $2 million and $5 million, the majority charged a fee between 0.8% to 1.0% for the portion of the portfolio over $2 million. Our example below will assume a 1% AUM fee.

Financial advisors often will only accept potential new clients if they have a minimum amount of assets to manage. In this example, we assume the client starts with $250,000 to be managed by a financial advisor charging 1% of AUM. This client contributes an inflation-adjusted $10,000 annually at the beginning of each year through age 64. I assume that in the first year, the $10,000 contribution brings the balance up to the $250,000 minimum required by the financial advisor. Assets are invested 70% in stocks (S&P 500) and 30% in bonds (10-year yields on US Treasury securities) with an overall expense ratio of 0.04%. The portfolio is rebalanced to 70% stocks and 30% bonds at the end of each year. I computed the following results, assuming a 30, 40, and 50 start age using Dr. Damodaran's data.

To start at 30, I examined the 62 sequences of 35-year durations from 1928 through 2023. Adjusting for inflation, the median real balance was $2,983,609 when the expense ratio was 0.04%. Including a 1% advisor fee increases the annual expense to 1.04%. This additional fee lowered the final account balance for each sequence by 22.0% to 25.3% or an inflation-adjusted amount of $375,869 to

$1,193,427. The median reduction was $695,872, enough to fund many years of retirement for the average American family.

Results from the 72 sequences of 25-year duration starting at age 40 showed this added fee lowered the median outcome by $316,424. The median percentage reduction in the final balance at age 65 was 17.9% for the 40-year-old start date and 11.4% for the 50-year-old start date.

Over an extended period, we can see the enormous impact of a small 1% fee. As expected, the percentage impact of this fee on the ending account balance grows more prominent the longer the investment time frame. Witness the power of compounding once again.

So far, we have only discussed the accumulation phase. What impact does an advisor fee have after you retire and are drawing down your portfolio for living expenses? One way to find an answer to this question is by looking at a widely used retirement planning rule of thumb. The 4% rule is attributed to retired financial advisor William Bengen, who wrote of it in the October 1994 article in the *Journal of Financial Planning.*[9]

The 4% rule says if you have a portfolio that is about 50% stocks and 50% intermediate US Treasuries, take 4% of your account balance in the first year of withdrawal and increase that amount for inflation every year; your portfolio should last 30 years with minimal fear of running out of money. For example, based on this rule of thumb, a person retiring at age 65 with $1.5 million can withdraw an inflation-adjusted $60,000 every year until age 95 and feel reasonably confident they will not outlive their portfolio. The 4% includes all outflows. An expense ratio is an example of an outflow. Advisor fees

9   Journal of Financial Planning. https://www.financialplanningassociation.org/sites/default/files/2021-04/MAR04%20Determining%20Withdrawal%20Rates%20Using%20Historical%20Data.pdf

are another. A meager expense ratio of 0.04% is only 1% of 4%. A 1% advisor fee would be 25% of 4%. If one used this rule of thumb in retirement and had a financial advisor charging 1% AUM in their first year of retirement, they would live on 3% of assets and pay the other 1% to their advisor. How do you feel about giving an advisor 25% of your money in your first year of retirement?

Hopefully, a financial advisor charging a 1% AUM fee would do much more than manage a two-fund portfolio. For example, they might advise a client whether they have saved enough to retire yet, help determine the best age to claim Social Security benefits, or develop a plan for drawing down their assets in retirement from different accounts in tax-efficient ways. Chapter 14 discusses the costs and benefits of financial advice, but for now, I want to you to be aware of the impact of AUM fees on a portfolio balance. If someone is being charged AUM fees for financial advice, they should know a seemingly small 1% fee can significantly impact their bottom line. All else being equal, if working with an advisor charging AUM fees, consider looking for someone charging sub-stantially less than 1% if they provide the services you need; such advisors who offer a holistic approach to retirement planning do exist.

CHAPTER 6

—

An Overview of Risk

DIFFERENT INVESTMENTS CARRY various levels and types of risk. Risk is an essential consideration when deciding which assets—and the percentage of your total portfolio—to invest in. Below is an introduction to measures of risk and return used in managing an investment portfolio.

Statistical Methods to Measure Risk

There are several ways to think about risk. Some use statistics to analyze historical data. Below are some statistics people may find helpful in understanding risk.

Simple Descriptive Statistics

When evaluating the risk of an investment or portfolio, it might be interesting to know the historical percentage of years with losses and the most significant annual loss. Vanguard provides a valuable overview of the returns for portfolios comprising stocks and bonds from 1926 through 2021 with its Model Portfolio Allocation. This overview shows the performance of stock and bond portfolios composed of 0%, 20%–80%, and 100% stocks with the remaining percentage in bonds. It reports the average annual return, the best year, the worst year, and the number of years with a loss for each asset allocation. Usually, asset allocations with more stocks and fewer bonds increase the number of times a loss occurs and increase the size of the most significant loss. A notable exception is moving from 0% stocks to 20% stocks; adding stocks lowered the number of years with a loss from 20 to 16. However, the biggest loss increased slightly, from 8.1% to 10.1%. Based on those two metrics, one might conclude risk remained the same, or maybe even decreased, by adding more of a riskier asset while improving the average annual rate of return from 6.3% to 7.5%. That result comes with diversification, discussed later in this chapter.

Another statistic often reported for an investment or entire portfolio is the standard deviation (σ). This statistic, which lets us know how much variation there is in the results, measures the total risk of an asset or an entire portfolio.

Calculating Risk-Adjusted Returns

People do not wish to take on additional risks without an incentive. That incentive is an expectation that, on average, a riskier investment will yield a higher rate of return than one that's less risky. But how can we compare different investments or different portfolios when their levels of risk are different? The answer is risk-adjusted returns. We first need to establish a baseline reference point, which is a risk-free rate of return—the reasonable expectation for the return on an investment with no risk. In finance, a proxy for this theoretical investment is often a 91-day Treasury bill; it's of short duration and considered to have an extremely low or zero default risk.

There are several ways to measure risk-adjusted returns but we will discuss just two of them. Perhaps the most used is the Sharpe ratio. Say you want to compare two potential investment portfolios based on past performance over some specified historical time frame. The Sharpe ratio would first compute the average rate of return for each portfolio (Rp) and subtract the risk-free rate of return (Rf). This provides a return on investment above what a risk-free investment yields. This result is then divided by the total variability for the portfolio (σ). The Sharpe ratio calculates the return above the risk-free rate per unit of the entire risk taken. It's a way to measure bang for your buck when taking on risk.

Variability includes both peaks and valleys. I don't know about you, but I am more concerned with the downside variability than the upside variability. Would you become worried if your portfolio shot up 30% next year? I didn't think so. The Sortino ratio is like the Sharpe ratio but different in one crucial way. While the Sharpe ratio calculates the return above the risk-free rate per unit of total risk taken, the Sortino ratio calculates the return above the risk-free rate per unit of downside risk taken (σd). I generally prefer this approach to measuring risk-adjusted returns.

One website popular with many do-it-yourself investors is Portfolio Visualizer.[10] While this website offers services for a fee, it provides a wealth of extensive statistical tools for free. With Portfolio Visualizer, one can back-test asset allocations or portfolios comprising specific stocks, mutual funds, or ETFs with data going back as far as 1972. One can examine the average rate of return for the portfolio or asset allocation, the standard deviation for the returns, the best year returns, the worst year returns, the maximum drawdown from peak to valley, the Sharpe ratio, and the Sortino ratio. It is one tool I have examined in developing my investment portfolio.

This section does not aim to provide an in-depth analysis of statistics but there are two main takeaways I wish for you: a general understanding of some statistics used to measure risk and a conceptual understanding of properly comparing different portfolios. Don't just look for the portfolio with the highest expected rate of return without considering risk. Instead, choose the best portfolio given the level of risk you're willing to take.

Sequence of Return Risk

Picture someone being informed of the average rate of return for their investment portfolio over the next 20-year investment time horizon. They even receive a list of annual returns, sorted from smallest to largest. You might think this information would tell a lot about how their portfolio would perform, but it might say very little because of the sequence of return risk. When making contributions before retire-

---

10   (Portfolio Visualizer) https://www.portfoliovisualizer.com/

ment or withdrawals during retirement, the order of returns can affect the outcome. Order wouldn't matter if there were no contributions or withdrawals in 20 years.

Sequence Risk During Accumulation

Let's examine the sequence of return risk before retirement by looking at the 20 years from 2000 through 2019. In Table 6.1, we consider a hypothetical person starting their journey to retirement. They ended the calendar year 1999 with $25,000 in invested assets. They will contribute additional money to invest at the start of each year for the next 20 years. In year one (2000), they invest an extra $10,000. Subsequently, they increased their contributions by the percentage increase in the Consumer Price Index for All Urban Consumers (CPI-U) in the prior year. In the middle of Table 6.1, you can find the rates of return for the S&P 500 and bonds (10-year US Treasury). I have assumed an expense ratio of 0.05% for the investments and rounded the actual annual averages net of these expenses to the nearest tenth of a percent. I have shown the historical results for three different asset allocations: 100% stocks, 50% stocks with the remaining 50% in bonds, and 100% bonds.

Table 6.1 Sequence 2000-2019, Accumulation Phase
$25,000 Starting Balance | $10,000 Real Contribution

Year	CPI-U	Deposit	Stocks	Bonds	Ending Balance (Stocks/Bonds)		
					100%/0%	50%/50%	0%/100%
2000	NA	10,000	-9.1%	16.6%	31,815	36,313	40,810
2001	2.6%	10,260	-11.9%	5.5%	37,068	45,082	53,879
2002	2.4%	10,506	-22.0%	15.1%	37,108	53,670	74,107
2003	1.4%	10,653	28.3%	0.3%	61,277	73,522	85,014
2004	1.8%	10,845	10.7%	4.4%	79,839	90,736	100,077
2005	2.2%	11,084	4.8%	2.8%	95,287	105,689	114,274
2006	2.5%	11,361	15.6%	1.9%	123,286	127,292	128,022
2007	2.3%	11,622	5.4%	10.2%	142,193	149,750	153,887
2008	2.3%	11,889	-36.6%	20.1%	97,688	148,304	199,097
2009	1.7%	12,091	25.9%	-11.2%	138,211	172,184	187,535
2010	1.0%	12,212	14.8%	8.4%	172,686	205,785	216,526
2011	1.7%	12,420	2.1%	16.0%	188,993	237,953	265,577
2012	2.1%	12,681	15.8%	2.9%	233,539	274,068	286,328
2013	1.8%	12,909	32.1%	-9.2%	325,558	319,836	271,707
2014	1.7%	13,128	13.5%	10.7%	384,408	373,253	315,312
2015	1.8%	13,364	1.3%	1.2%	402,943	391,450	332,620
2016	2.2%	13,658	11.7%	0.6%	465,344	430,022	348,356
2017	1.8%	13,904	21.6%	2.8%	582,765	498,085	372,403
2018	2.1%	14,196	-4.3%	-0.1%	571,292	501,010	386,213
2019	2.2%	14,508	31.2%	9.6%	768,569	620,684	439,190

Sources:
pages.stern.nyu.edu/~adamodar/New_Home_Page/datafile/histretSP.html
US Bureau of Labor Statistics, CPI-U, Series ID number CUUR0000SA0L1E

Before we examine the importance of the sequence of returns, it's worth noting that during this period, bonds were very good at providing diversification. It is often said that bonds are more for safety than their returns. Stocks plummeted in 2000–2002, losing over 35% of their value, and experienced another 36% drop in 2008. During each of those four years, bonds had favorable rates of return. Three out of four years saw bond returns exceeding 15%. Do bonds always have a positive return when stocks get hammered? Unfortunately, the answer is no. In 2022, when the S&P 500 was down 18%, 10-year US Treasuries also lost about 17.8%. That said, stocks and bonds rarely have a strong positive correlation. Bonds in a portfolio often help cushion the blow of significant stock losses.

As noted above, bonds did much better in 2000 through 2002 than stocks. A 100% stock allocation would have yielded a balance of $37,108 by the end of 2002. While the investment received an additional contribution of $30,766 over three years, the final balance only grew by $12,108. With a 100% bond allocation, the balance would have nearly doubled to $74,107 after three years, outperforming the 100% stock portfolio. Step into the shoes of a young investor whose investments are solely in stocks. Would you have been tempted to withdraw your money from stocks until things seemed "safe" again? If you had stayed the course with a 100% stock portfolio for the first nine years, you would have weathered the Great Recession. Over those nine years, you would have contributed an additional $98,220, ending with a balance of only $97,688. Meanwhile, a 100% bond allocation over these nine years would have resulted in a balance of almost $200,000. Imagine how you would feel. Are you still determined to stick with the current course of action? The losses endured in the stock market during 2008 caused many to sell their investments and move to cash. I know some people knowledgeable about personal finance did so; they were just overcome with fear and misjudged their risk tolerance.

The stock investor would find the next 11 years much more delightful. After only five additional years, the balance on the 100% stock portfolio would be larger than the 100% bond portfolio. At the end of 20 years, the 100% stock portfolio would provide a balance of $768,569, 175% of the 100% bond portfolio.

Table 6.2 presents the results with the order of the returns reversed. So, 2019 is year number one, 2018 is year number two, etc. I flip the order for the inflation adjustments to keep the overall contribution increases the same. With no additional contributions, Table 6.1 and Table 6.2 would end up with the same final balances after 20 years. That is not the case when adding new contributions.

Recall in Table 6.1 the final balance after 20 years in the 100% stock portfolio was 175% of the 100% bond portfolio. Reversing the order of the returns has the 100% bond portfolio ahead. Why did this happen? No one likes significant percentage losses when investing, but if it must happen, it is better when you have relatively little money at stake. Stocks did poorly in 2000, 2001, and 2002. In Table 6.2, those are the last three years. After the first 17 years, as shown in Table 6.2, the 100% stock portfolio is ahead of the 100% bond portfolio by what seems to be a large margin. The stock portfolio had a balance of 175% of the bond portfolio. However, the significant losses for stocks in the last three years and the solid performance of bonds during that time produced considerable change in what might seem like a short period. After 20 years, the bond portfolio ends with a balance of $527,137, while the stock portfolio ends with only $397,713.

Table 6.2 Reverse Sequence 2019-2000, Accumulation Phase
$25,000 Starting Balance | $10,000 Real Contribution

Year	CPI-U	Deposit	Stocks	Bonds	Ending Balance (Stocks/Bonds)		
					100%/0%	50%/50%	0%/100%
2019	NA	10,000	31.2%	9.6%	45,920	42,140	38,360
2018	2.2%	10,220	-4.3%	-0.1%	53,726	51,208	48,531
2017	2.1%	10,435	21.6%	2.8%	78,020	69,164	60,617
2016	1.8%	10,623	11.7%	0.6%	99,014	84,693	71,668
2015	2.2%	10,857	1.3%	1.2%	111,299	96,745	83,515
2014	1.8%	11,052	13.5%	10.7%	138,869	120,840	104,686
2013	1.7%	11,240	32.1%	-9.2%	198,294	147,203	105,261
2012	1.8%	11,442	15.8%	2.9%	242,874	173,479	120,087
2011	2.1%	11,682	2.1%	16.0%	259,901	201,918	152,852
2010	1.7%	11,881	14.8%	8.4%	312,006	238,599	178,571
2009	1.0%	12,000	25.9%	-11.2%	407,924	269,018	169,227
2008	1.7%	12,204	-36.6%	20.1%	266,361	258,022	217,898
2007	2.3%	12,485	5.4%	10.2%	293,904	291,606	253,883
2006	2.3%	12,772	15.6%	1.9%	354,517	331,011	271,721
2005	2.5%	13,091	4.8%	2.8%	385,253	357,178	292,787
2004	2.2%	13,379	10.7%	4.4%	441,286	398,534	319,637
2003	1.8%	13,620	28.3%	0.3%	**583,644**	**471,092**	**334,257**
2002	1.4%	13,811	-22.0%	15.1%	466,015	468,174	400,626
2001	2.4%	14,142	-11.9%	5.5%	423,019	466,882	437,580
2000	2.6%	14,510	-9.1%	16.6%	**397,713**	**499,444**	**527,137**

Sources:
pages.stern.nyu.edu/~adamodar/New_Home_Page/datafile/histretSP.html
US Bureau of Labor Statistics, CPI-U, Series ID number CUUR0000SA0L1E

A key point here: Volatility during the accumulation phase is more dangerous when you are dealing with significant amounts of money and have relatively little time left before needing to rely on your account balance to support your lifestyle. The sequence of return risk is higher the closer you are to the finish line. This is one reason target retirement date mutual funds have lower percentages of stocks as the target date gets closer.

Sequence Risk During Withdrawal

Now, let's imagine someone at the beginning of retirement who starts withdrawing from their investment accounts.

This investor ended the calendar year 1999 with $1 million in invested assets. For the next 20 years, they will withdraw all the money they need for living expenses at the start of each year. They will follow the 4% rule for their withdrawal strategy. So, in year one (2000), they withdrew $40,000, 4% of their initial balance. In subsequent years, they increased their withdrawals by the percentage increase in the CPI-U in the prior year. The other assumptions about investment returns and expense ratios remain the same as in Tables 6.1 and 6.2.

Table 6.3 contains the results for the sequence from 2000 through 2019. Think about how you might feel in this retiree's shoes after the first three years. If you had invested 100% in stocks during the first three years, your nest egg would have almost halved, with many more years of retirement ahead. Would you feel a lot of worry and anxiety? I think I would. What about the 50/50 portfolio, which closes out the first three years with a balance of $851,934? Does the balance drop of about 15% over three years concern you? If so, how concerned are you about it?

Table 6.3 Sequence 2000-2019, Withdrawal Phase
$1,000,000 Starting Balance | $40,000 Real Withdrawal

Year	CPI-U	Withdraw	Stocks	Bonds	Ending Balance (Stocks/Bonds) 100%/0%	50%/50%	0%/100%
2000	NA	40,000	-9.1%	16.6%	872,640	996,000	1,119,360
2001	2.6%	41,040	-11.9%	5.5%	732,640	924,401	1,137,628
2002	2.4%	42,025	-22.0%	15.1%	538,679	851,934	1,261,039
2003	1.4%	42,613	28.3%	0.3%	636,453	925,054	1,222,081
2004	1.8%	43,380	10.7%	4.4%	656,532	948,241	1,230,564
2005	2.2%	44,334	4.8%	2.8%	641,584	938,255	1,219,444
2006	2.5%	45,442	15.6%	1.9%	689,140	970,934	1,196,308
2007	2.3%	46,487	5.4%	10.2%	677,356	996,554	1,267,103
2008	2.3%	47,556	-36.6%	20.1%	399,293	870,706	1,464,676
2009	1.7%	48,364	25.9%	-11.2%	441,820	882,784	1,257,685
2010	1.0%	48,848	14.8%	8.4%	451,132	930,672	1,310,379
2011	1.7%	49,678	2.1%	16.0%	409,884	960,724	1,462,413
2012	2.1%	50,721	15.8%	2.9%	415,911	995,089	1,452,632
2013	1.8%	51,634	32.1%	-9.2%	481,210	1,051,480	1,272,106
2014	1.7%	52,512	13.5%	10.7%	486,572	1,119,844	1,350,090
2015	1.8%	53,457	1.3%	1.2%	438,745	1,079,716	1,312,193
2016	2.2%	54,633	11.7%	0.6%	429,054	1,088,126	1,265,105
2017	1.8%	55,616	21.6%	2.8%	454,100	1,158,476	1,243,355
2018	2.1%	56,784	-4.3%	-0.1%	380,231	1,077,455	1,185,384
2019	2.2%	58,033	31.2%	9.6%	422,724	1,227,384	1,235,577

Sources:
pages.stern.nyu.edu/~adamodar/New_Home_Page/datafile/histretSP.html
US Bureau of Labor Statistics, CPI-U, Series ID number CUUR0000SA0L1E

The other gut check comes in 2008 if you were not 100% in bonds. For the 100% stock portfolio, there was a general rebound in the portfolio balance after 2002, but *devastating* might be the right word to describe 2008. Between the end of 2007 and the end of 2008, the 100% stock portfolio balance dropped by about 39%, from $677,356 to $399,293. You would have less than 40% of the money you started with after just nine years. I think that would cause most people to panic. This is especially true during the withdrawal phase when you see your balance shrink while simultaneously needing to withdraw money for living expenses. It is truly a double whammy.

You have probably heard the saying it is best to "buy low and sell high." Being forced to sell low is a headwind encountered by a portfolio trying to bounce back after a significant loss. If you were in the 50/50 portfolio, bonds helped cushion the blow of 2008; they experienced their best return in the 20 years we are examining. The 50/50 portfolio dropped about 13% in 2008 from $996,554 to $870,706. Would that cause you anxiety? If so, how much anxiety? Would the portfolio's performance tempt you to adjust your asset allocation? There is no right or wrong answer to these questions. We all have different levels of risk aversion.

At the end of 20 years, the 50/50 and 100% bond portfolios have approximately the same amount of money. The 100% stock portfolio comes in a distant third place with only about one-third of the balance of the other two portfolios.

Now, let's reverse the sequence of events and see what changes. Table 6.4 shows what a strong tailwind for stocks early in retirement can do. The first 11 years for stocks produce generally strong returns with no significant drops in value. The 100% stock portfolio more than tripled over the first 11 years despite the annual withdrawals for living expenses. Even after the Great Recession in 2008, the ending balance is more than twice where it started. Despite significant losses in the last three years, this portfolio remains on top after 20 years because of the substantial headwind it generated.

Table 6.4 Reverse Sequence 2019–2000, Withdrawal Phase
$1,000,000 Starting Balance | $40,000 Real Withdrawal

Year	CPI-U	Withdraw	Stocks	Bonds	Ending Balance (Stocks/Bonds) 100%/0%	50%/50%	0%/100%
2019	NA	40,000	31.2%	9.6%	1,259,520	1,155,840	1,052,160
2018	2.2%	40,880	-4.3%	-0.1%	1,166,238	1,090,431	1,010,269
2017	2.1%	41,738	21.6%	2.8%	1,367,393	1,176,633	995,650
2016	1.8%	42,489	11.7%	0.6%	1,479,917	1,203,894	958,880
2015	2.2%	43,424	1.3%	1.2%	1,455,168	1,174,976	926,441
2014	1.8%	44,206	13.5%	10.7%	1,601,442	1,267,593	976,634
2013	1.7%	44,958	32.1%	-9.2%	2,056,115	1,362,627	845,962
2012	1.8%	45,767	15.8%	2.9%	2,327,983	1,439,987	823,401
2011	2.1%	46,728	2.1%	16.0%	2,329,161	1,519,348	900,940
2010	1.7%	47,522	14.8%	8.4%	2,619,322	1,642,558	925,105
2009	1.0%	47,997	25.9%	-11.2%	3,237,298	1,711,762	778,872
2008	1.7%	48,813	-36.6%	20.1%	2,021,499	1,525,755	876,801
2007	2.3%	49,936	5.4%	10.2%	2,078,028	1,590,933	911,205
2006	2.3%	51,085	15.6%	1.9%	2,343,146	1,674,585	876,463
2005	2.5%	52,362	4.8%	2.8%	2,400,741	1,683,867	847,175
2004	2.2%	53,514	10.7%	4.4%	2,598,381	1,753,445	828,583
2003	1.8%	54,477	28.3%	0.3%	3,263,829	1,941,921	776,428
2002	1.4%	55,240	-22.0%	15.1%	2,502,699	1,821,590	830,087
2001	2.4%	56,566	-11.9%	5.5%	2,155,043	1,708,543	816,065
2000	2.6%	58,037	-9.1%	16.6%	1,906,179	1,712,400	883,861

Sources:
pages.stern.nyu.edu/~adamodar/New_Home_Page/datafile/histretSP.html
US Bureau of Labor Statistics, CPI-U, Series ID number CUUR0000SA0L1E

We can't know how well stocks will perform in the early retirement years until that time comes and goes but the sequence of return risk should be a significant concern for many recent retirees. While in the accumulation phase, you may work a few extra years if the market has produced poor results. For many people, the instant they retire, their earning capacity significantly depreciates, akin to driving a brand-new car off the showroom floor. If the early retirement years yield solid returns, this risk will be less of a concern. However, if the first retirement years are rocky, stock-heavy portfolios could be subject to considerable sequence risk. Investors should note this danger and invest according to their ability, need, and willingness to take risks.

One last thing before moving on: Some may believe it is safe to set a withdrawal rate equal to the average investment return minus an assumed average inflation rate. For example, for the historical period we examined, the arithmetic average rate of return for the S&P 500 was 7.5%, and inflation averaged 2.0%. If the S&P 500 returned exactly 7.5% yearly and inflation was 2.0% each year, one could sustain a 5.5% withdrawal rate indefinitely. What would have happened in Table 6.3 if the withdrawal rate changed from 4% to 5.5%? The portfolio would have run out of money in 2014. A reasonable withdrawal rate can't only consider average returns and ignore downside volatility.

Answering the Big Picture Questions

Risk may refer to more than just the ups and downs of an investment or an entire portfolio. It may refer to the objectives of the portfolio. Many nearing retirement worry most about the lifespan of their portfolio; will they outlive their retirement investments? Because of this concern, many people nearing retirement encounter the one-more-year syndrome. If they work *just one more year*, they think they will be able to retire and feel much more confident about the long-term survival of their investment portfolio and its ability to provide for their wants and needs. The following year, with significant continued anxiety, many repeat this cycle. Some people may work the same full-time job five or even 10 years longer but others hate their job and wish to retire as soon as possible. What about the risk of working longer than necessary for their financial wants and needs?

Is it possible to find answers to these critical questions using statistics? It is, at least to a certain extent. While stats cannot give definite answers, they can provide reasonable estimates of the likelihood of certain events based on underlying assumptions. Historical data can reveal the frequency of past events. Another statistical tool used by professionals and do-it-yourself investors is Monte Carlo simulations. The simulations rely on estimated average returns and standard deviations for different investment types. The averages and standard deviations may be based on historical outcomes or future forecasts. While either method may provide reassurance when tackling these vital questions, the future is still unpredictable.

Measuring Your Risk Tolerance

In Chapter 1, I mentioned how exposure to lists could uncover blind spots in your game plan. Similarly, thinking about questions involving risk-taking may produce additional self-awareness. I believe many people overestimate their risk tolerance. I hope you reflected on your feelings in various hypothetical circumstances as we looked at the sequence of return risk. Looking at drops in a hypothetical portfolio balance is one thing but it's quite another experience when it is your money! Many studies attempt to measure risk tolerance and professionally crafted surveys that dive deeper into the subject are worth looking at. I took one that required no personal information; the results are recorded anonymously.[11]

CHAPTER 7

—

Control What You Can During Accumulation

UNTIL NOW, WE have focused on some obstacles faced during the journey to retirement: Cognitive blind spots and biases that can contribute to poor financial choices. Those lacking knowledge of compounding and risk may decide against their self-interest. Armed with knowledge and awareness of these obstacles, we are ready to examine the choices we can make while in the accumulation phase.

Time in the Market

The initial decision is when to start. In Chapter 5, we examined the example of Jim, 25 years old and new to investing. Jim had just started a job with a salary of $50,000 and invested 20% of his salary, including a 5% employer match, in a company-provided 401(k) plan. We looked at the historical performance of investing in an index fund tracking the S&P 500 starting at different ages. As you may recall, delaying contribution to the company plan by five years resulted in a considerable reduction in the median historical outcome. That's the power of compounding in action. If Jim wanted the same results but started five years later, he would have to increase his contribution rate significantly. Would that extra future savings burden be larger or smaller than the benefit of a higher immediate spending budget for the first five years? Analyzing past results facilitates educated decisions in these types of situations.

We have also seen that outcomes can vary significantly based on the existing market returns while we are investing. How we invest plays a role in the results we will see. Unfortunately, there is another uncontrollable factor: the year we were born. The year we were born has far-reaching implications. It defines the market's state in your 20s, 30s, and so on. Your investments may not meet expectations partly because of the period you lived through. Unless someone cannot work because of a disability, they can increase their accumulation phase by working and contributing to their retirement fund for more years. The next section discusses an alternative for someone in this situation.

Rate of Savings

If your nest egg is growing slower than you had hoped, increasing your savings rate by cutting spending may be another option. Again, time in the market is generally your friend while in the accumulation phase. Higher savings rates early in the accumulation phase give compound growth more time to work its magic. The rate of savings will vary by household.

Some questions to ask when determining a savings rate for you or your household: What are your saving objectives? Is the primary goal to retire early? The earlier you plan to tap into your nest egg, the more you will probably need in it. Are you open to working part-time in retirement? If so, that may provide more options. What flexibility do you have with discretionary spending before retirement? Does your savings rate balance the desire for current spending and the lower value of your estimated nest egg?

Investment Asset Allocation

Time in the market and savings rates will affect the balance of the portfolio you take into the withdrawal phase. How you invest your money will also play a role. Let's begin by examining historical outcomes for US stock and bond allocations using Dr. Damodaran's data and how they may affect early and later portions of the accumulation phase.

US Stocks (S&P 500) vs. US Bonds (10-Year Treasury)

We will examine historical outcomes assuming a 30-year invest-ment horizon. Table 7.1 considers the early part of this period. The top portion considers a 30-year investment horizon, starting with an investment balance of zero. The investor allocates a contribution inflation-adjusted amount of $10,000 each year to one of five different asset allocations in this table. These allocations include 100%, 80%, 60%, 40%, or 20% stocks, with the remaining percentage invested in bonds. The bottom half of Table 7.1 assumes a starting balance of $200,000 after 10 years of investing, with 20 years remaining in the accumulation phase. Table 7.2 examines the last 10 and five years of this period with assumed starting balances of $500,000 after 20 years and $850,000 after 25 years. Investments are made in indices reflect-ing these two investments with a portfolio expense ratio of 0.05%.

Table 7.1 Historic Stock / Bond Allocation Outcomes Early During Accumulation

30-Year Horizon, $0 Starting Balance | $10,000 Real Contributions Per Year

Percentile	100% / 0%	80% / 20%	60% / 40%	40% / 60%	20% / 80%
Median	1,031,303	954,729	838,990	628,831	474,494
10th	592,180	527,627	441,010	373,841	319,525
5th	535,781	463,685	397,254	346,703	298,232
Lowest	459,581	396,820	338,473	285,916	239,754

20-Year Horizon, $200,000 Starting Balance | $10,000 Real Contributions Per Year

Percentile	100% / 0%	80% / 20%	60% / 40%	40% / 60%	20% / 80%
Median	1,250,649	1,058,019	925,894	770,426	576,411
10th	571,564	530,716	506,657	455,418	403,144
5th	515,127	496,724	453,871	415,095	375,819
Lowest	428,190	400,491	368,320	333,161	296,458

Conventional wisdom says to invest heavily in stocks instead of bonds if the investment horizon is long. Considering all 30- and 20-year sequences from 1928 through 2023, the 100% stock portfolio would have performed the best at all percentiles. Even in terrible market conditions, if someone stuck with the same asset allocation for 20 or 30 years, the 100% stock portfolio would have performed the best.

Should everyone with over 20 years left to invest focus solely on stocks? I believe the answer is no. First, past performance guarantees nothing about future performance. Don't assume something won't happen just because it hasn't happened yet. Chapter 6 examined the reverse sequence from 2019 to 2000 during a 20-year accumulation phase. Having some bonds during that time would have been beneficial if that sequence had occurred. Second, a 100% stock portfolio is likely to be volatile. Many would find the bumpy ride quite anxiety-inducing and could lead some who invested 100% in stocks to switch strategies when it got tough and either add more bonds to their portfolio for perceived additional safety or go to cash holdings. Selling low is often a result of fear, which is likely why someone gets out of stocks after a prolonged decline. Greed is another emotion that can cause bad financial decisions. We discuss that in more detail shortly.

**Table 7.2 Historic Stock / Bond Allocation
Outcomes Late During Accumulation**

10-Year Horizon, $500,000 Starting Balance | $10,000 Real Contributions Per Year

Percentile	100% / 0%	80% / 20%	60% / 40%	40% / 60%	20% / 80%
Median	1,110,573	1,057,604	965,408	901,694	792,982
10th	548,761	565,733	581,326	554,650	523,973
5th	476,706	501,805	520,350	510,260	500,377
Lowest	400,749	428,122	452,511	439,932	408,179

5-Year Horizon, $850,000 Starting Balance | $10,000 Real Contributions Per Year

Percentile	100% / 0%	80% / 20%	60% / 40%	40% / 60%	20% / 80%
Median	1,322,494	1,272,047	1,165,376	1,093,524	1,050,188
10th	761,058	799,895	850,063	842,378	813,575
5th	648,205	776,189	789,704	792,293	783,573
Lowest	526,765	602,107	679,361	692,335	645,729

Table 7.2 presents the results with 10 or five years remaining during the accumulation phase. The portfolio's heavy lifting in the last 10 years primarily comes from the starting balance of $500,000, which considerably exceeds the $100,000 inflation-adjusted contributions made during that time. As expected, the median result grows as the percentage invested in stock rises. However, we see the value of bonds protecting us from downside risk with 10 years left in the accumulation phase. Dropping from 100% stocks to 80% stocks to 60% stocks, the median outcome declines from $1,110,573 to $1,057,604 to $965,408, respectively. However, the 10th percentile, 5th percentile, and lowest outcome increase with the addition of bonds. The 10th percentile outcomes increase from $548,761 to $565,733 to $581,326, the 5th percentile outcomes increase from $476,706 to $501,805 to $520,350, and the lowest historical outcome increases from $400,749 to $428,122 to $452,511. The portfolios with 40% stocks and 20% stocks historically underperformed the other three

asset allocations at each percentile examined. How much lower of a median result would you accept for improved outcomes when the market has poor results? There is no correct answer, only the one right for your risk tolerance.

Investing 100% in stocks with only five years remaining in the accumulation phase appears risky. Starting with $850,000 and contributing an additional $50,000 over the final five years resulted in an inflation-adjusted balance of only $761,058 or less in 10% of the cases. Adding bonds historically lowered the median outcome but added protection to downside volatility. Dropping from 100% stocks to 80% stocks to 60% stocks to 40% stocks, the median outcome declines from $1,322,494 to $1,272,047 to $1,165,376 to $1,093,524, respectively. The 100% stock portfolio produced the lowest outcomes at the 10th percentile and 5th percentile, and had the lowest overall outcome. The 10th percentile, 5th percentile, and lowest outcome with the 100% stock portfolio were $761,058, $648,205, and $526,765. The 10th percentile results for the 80/20, 60/40, and 40/60 portfolios were $799,895, $850,063, and $842,378. The 5th percentile results were $776,189, $789,704, and $792,293 with the lowest results being $602,107, $679,361, and $692,355. The two asset allocations that performed best at the bottom end of the distribution were 60/40 and 40/60. The 20% stock portfolio underperformed the 40% stock portfolio at each percentile examined. Which allocation at the five-year mark would best suit your risk tolerance? Does this allocation have more bonds in it than your selection at the 10-year mark? People are typically less tolerant of risk as their retirement age approaches, but everyone's risk tolerance is unique.

Imagine a scenario where stocks had performed exceptionally well in recent years as you approach the final five years of the accumulation phase. Your account balance is more significant than you had expected. Would that influence your asset allocation? Would recent market outcomes tempt you to increase the percentage of stocks in your portfolio? Or perhaps your need to take risks would be lower and you would adjust your asset allocation to be more conservative. Awareness of your tendencies, values, and potential biases is beneficial in helping you make the right decision.

Domestic (Us) Vs. International Stocks

So far, we have focused on the S&P 500, or its estimated equivalent, when discussing stocks due to the public availability of data. Actual data for long-term stock market returns for countries outside the United States are not nearly as accessible, at least not for free. Proprietary data—the Dimson-Marsh-Staunton dataset—exists for many countries going back as far as 1900 and you can subscribe to this data by contacting Morningstar, Inc. You can also purchase a 272-page book, *The Credit Suisse International Investments Returns Yearbook 2023*, which provides information on historical stock market returns for many countries dating back to 1900.

Fortunately, a free publication for those wishing to learn more about long-term stock market performance outside the United States contains excerpts from the abovementioned book. *The Credit Suisse International Investment Returns Yearbook 2023 Summary Edition* was written by Elroy Dimson, Paul Marsh, and Mike Staunton.[12] You may wish to read or at least skim this publication if are contemplating how you should weight international stocks in your investment portfolio.

---

12   Studies & publications — Credit Suisse. credit-suisse.com

Do you need international stocks to have a well-diversified portfolio? Some respected investors have given a firm no as the answer. These include John "Jack" Bogle, the founder of The Vanguard Group, and Warren Buffett chairman and CEO of Berkshire Hathaway. In a 2013 letter to the shareholders of Berkshire Hathaway, Warren Buffett revealed some advice he gave to the trustee of his will: Investments for his wife's benefit should be 90% in a very low-cost S&P 500 index fund with 10% in short-term government bonds.[13]

Our economy is increasingly international. One argument for a US investor not needing international stocks for a well-diversified portfolio is the worldwide outreach of large US companies. Investing in the S&P 500 or a total US market index fund will incorporate the business activity of these firms beyond American borders. Another argument is that investing in foreign companies introduces exchange rate risk. For example, a US investor purchases $1,000 worth of a mutual fund of European companies. Any change in the exchange rate between the euro and the US dollar between the time of purchase and the time of sale will affect the investor's profit (or loss) when the mutual fund is sold. This increases the uncertainty and risk associated with purchasing stocks.

Since 1900, the US has, on average, outperformed the rest of the international economy. The US holds more than half of the worldwide stock market's value. Is there any reason to invest in international stocks if you are a US investor? Perhaps despite increasing internationalization, investing in foreign companies still provides some diversification benefits.

13   https://www.berkshirehathaway.com/letters/2013ltr.pdf

Some question whether the US will continue its hot streak in the decades to come. Let's look at the historic performance of two index funds from Vanguard: the Vanguard Total International Stock Index Fund (VTSMX) and the Vanguard Total Stock Market Index Fund (VGTSX). I chose these specific funds because of the length of their historical returns. I found returns for these mutual funds from 1997 through 2022 at Yahoo Finance (Stock Market Live, Quotes, Business & Finance News). Using the annual rate of returns for each mutual fund, I estimated the return on a $10,000 investment made in each mutual fund at the end of 1996. While 1997 was an exceptional year for US stocks, it wasn't so much for international stocks. US stocks increased by about 31% that year; international stocks lost less than 1%. However, international stocks did better than US stocks for the six years from 2002 through 2007. At the end of the 11 years from 1997 through 2007, the international stock fund would have approximately $24,452, and the US stock fund was about $24,010. What would have resulted if someone had invested $10,000 in each fund at the end of 2007? By the end of 2022, the US fund would have exceeded the international mutual fund by over 270%, totaling around $34,454, compared to $12,679. Are US stocks overvalued compared to international stocks? That may be the case despite—or perhaps because—many expect international stocks to outperform US stocks over the next decade. Time will reveal the uncertain future performance of international and US stocks.

Other Investments

Above, we discussed the inclusion of US bonds, US stocks, and international stocks in a well-diversified portfolio. Some choose to include other investments or outweigh certain stocks in their portfolio and I will mention some alternatives, but the purpose of this book is not to provide recommendations for an investment portfolio.

One familiar investment people include in their assets is real estate. This often is rental property the investor owns. Another common way to own real estate is to purchase mutual funds or ETF real estate investment trusts (REITs). Many people investing in real estate prefer REITs because they do not require property management or maintenance. REITs are also more diversified and a more liquid asset. If you invest in a total US market mutual fund or ETF, you own some real estate. Some people choose to overweight real estate in their portfolios as a hedge against inflation. Others mention that some types of real estate are not publicly traded. So, a total market index fund is under-weighting real estate.

Small capitalization value companies are another portion of the total stock market where portfolios are sometimes overweight. Historically, small-cap value stocks have outperformed the market over long periods but may underperform the market for over a decade and exhibit more volatility than the S&P 500. Paul Merriman, a retired financial advisor and current financial educator, has long been a vocal proponent of investing in small-cap value stocks. He is the founder of The Merriman Financial Education Foundation. His website, Paul Merriman, offers additional information about small-cap value stocks, including a comparison in performance between US small-cap value stocks and the S&P 500 dating back to 1928.[14]

Investors sometimes include precious metals like gold in a well-diversified portfolio. One nice feature about gold is the

14   Paul Merriman. https://paulmerriman.com/

low correlation it has had historically with stocks. For this reason, investors sometimes include this asset for safety from significant market downturns.

The last investment I will mention here is cryptocurrency. This investment is highly volatile, with a relatively brief history. If you detect I am not a fan of investing in cryptocurrencies, you are not wrong. Investing in crypto may be the best thing since sliced bread. However, from December 10, 2017 to December 9, 2018, Bitcoin lost about 83% of its value, and from November 7, 2021 to November 6, 2022, it lost a little over 75% of its value! The downside volatility is too high for my tastes, but others may disagree.

Asset Location

Besides deciding what assets to invest in, you must determine which accounts to place your investments in. One type is tax-deferred and includes traditional individual retirement accounts (IRAs) and employer-provided plans, like a traditional 401(k), 403(b), or 457 plans. Contributions to these accounts lower your taxable income, and you pay taxes when you sell the investments. Individuals contribute after-tax money to Roth variants for these types of investments and can make tax-free withdrawals without penalty if specific requirements are met.

To Roth or not to Roth? That is the question many people contemplate. *Should I forgo a tax break today for tax-free withdrawals years later?* Hopefully, the magic of compound growth has done its thing. *Or should I take the tax break now and pay taxes later at ordinary income tax rates?* One consideration is your current income level versus your expected future income. The Roth option should generally be more enticing at the beginning of an individual's time in the labor market than later as the benefit of the tax break is typically the lowest when you are young with little labor market experience. When young, you also have more time for compound growth to work its magic before withdrawing. Most workers earn more as they age and gain additional labor market experience. As this happens, the tax break benefit for contributing to a traditional tax-deferred account becomes more valuable. Of course, all of this is a broad generalization. Other things to consider include the tax bracket you expect to be in at retirement. Unexpected changes in marginal tax brackets may also occur, complicating the decision between Roth and traditional contributions.

There are income limits for those wishing to contribute to a Roth IRA. In 2024, single and head-of-household tax filers could contribute to a Roth IRA if their modified adjusted gross income (MAGI) was less than $161,000; $240,000 for those married and filing jointly. In 2024, single tax filers received no tax deduction for contributions to a traditional IRA if their income was at least $87,000. The figure was $143,000 for those married and filing jointly.

If you surpass these limits, there might be an alternative way to contribute to a Roth IRA if you have earned income. You might not qualify for a tax break if your income is too high. The backdoor Roth contribution starts with a non-tax-deductible contribution to a traditional IRA. After depositing the money in the traditional IRA, individuals roll over the funds to a Roth IRA. This strategy works best if you start the process with a balance of zero in all traditional IRAs you might own. Pro rata taxation may apply to the rollover if you have other traditional IRA money. If you think a backdoor Roth contribution may make sense, please consult an advisor or tax professional.

Another type of account is a taxable brokerage account. Investors put money into these accounts after paying taxes and face the capital gains tax rate on any long-term gains when they sell investments in these accounts. For most, the long-term capital gains tax rate is 0% or 15%. In 2024, if taxable income was up to $47,025 for single filers or $94,050 for married persons filing jointly, the long-term capital tax rate was 0%. The long-term capital tax rate in 2024 was 15% for taxable income between $47,025 and $518,900 for single filers, and $94,050 and $583,750 for married persons filing jointly. Short-term capital gains tax rates apply for investments held for less than a year, the same as ordinary income. You can also receive income in a taxable account without selling an asset. Except for municipal bonds, interest income from bonds and dividends are subject to federal taxes.

How do you choose which of these three accounts to invest in? While each situation is unique, here are some factors to consider. The first step is to consider grabbing any employer match. Regardless of how terrible the investments offered in your employer's retirement plan options may be, it is typically a good idea to contribute enough money at least to get any match—free money—they offer. If they offered a dollar-for-dollar match, that is an instant 100% rate of return. It's hard to beat that!

Suppose you are married and filing jointly in 2024. You and your spouse both work full-time with $175,000 in combined income. What should be your next move? Here, the choice would be easy for many investing with a long-term aim: Roth IRA contributions for you and your spouse. Why? Your income would be too high to contribute to a deductible traditional IRA. You could invest in a traditional IRA without a tax deduction, but you and your spouse could still make Roth IRA contributions. It is better to pay no taxes when you withdraw your money down the road from a Roth IRA than paying ordinary income tax rates after withdrawing from a traditional IRA. In this example, a long-term buy-and-hold investor would generally prefer a Roth IRA over a taxable account because it allows reinvestment of dividends or interest without immediate or future tax obligations.

We briefly mentioned the choice between traditional and Roth contributions. How about brokerage accounts that are subject to taxes? Investors can access these accounts without facing early withdrawal penalties that may apply to IRAs and employer-sponsored retirement plans; this flexibility may be useful for those wishing to retire before age 59½. Capital gains tax rates may also be less than ordinary income tax rates associated with traditional IRAs and employer-sponsored plans. As mentioned earlier, one of the wild cards while investing during the accumulation stage is unknown future changes to tax rates. Investing money in different accounts with different associated tax rates allows for tax diversification.

Besides deciding which accounts to invest your money in, you must also determine which investments in your portfolio will go into each type of investment account. The asset allocation doesn't have to be the same in every account. What matters is the asset allocation for your overall portfolio. So how do you make this choice? Every situation is unique, but below is some general advice many financial advisors may provide.

As mentioned earlier, interest income and dividends may be distributed periodically. In a tax-deferred account, you can reinvest them with no tax consequences. Inside a taxable brokerage account, they can generate a taxable event. For this reason, many financial advisors recommend placing tax-efficient investments, such as US total stock market index funds or S&P 500 index funds, in a taxable brokerage account if you have one. Traditional IRA and employer-sponsored plans are tax-deferred, so periodic interest and dividend distributions are not a tax concern in these accounts. Withdrawals are subject to ordinary income tax rates, which may be higher than long-term capital gains tax rates, so placing tax-inefficient investments with low expected growth rates in these accounts may be a good decision. Bonds are tax-inefficient and, on average, have grown slower than stocks. Investments in a Roth account can escape taxes if distributions meet some requirements. Many financial advisors recommend placing assets with a high expected growth rate in these accounts. This is often considered an excellent place to invest in stocks.

Portfolio Complexity

How many mutual funds or ETFs do you need for a well-diversified portfolio? The answer is at least one. One ETF or mutual fund might be the right solution for you. Examples of a well-diversified one-fund portfolio are target date, balanced, or lifestyle funds. Target date funds have a glide path for stock and bond allocations, becoming more conservative as the target date approaches. Low-cost index-based target date funds are available from places like Schwab, Fidelity, and Vanguard. Index-based target date funds that are not actively managed should have less than 0.2% expense ratios. There are index funds with expense ratios much more significant than 0.2%, but those are actively managed. Balanced and lifestyle funds maintain a constant asset allocation. For example, if you wanted an asset allocation with approximately 80% stocks and 20% bonds, one option might be Vanguard's LifeStrategy® Growth Fund.

Let's examine the pros and cons of having a straightforward one-fund portfolio. One pro is rebalancing. You never have to do it. A one-fund portfolio is the ultimate set-it-and-forget-it portfolio. It may reduce impulses to tweak your asset allocation, protecting you from yourself. Are you concerned about your spouse's ability to handle family finances after you're gone, especially if they're not interested in finance? Perhaps you are worried about cognitive decline as you get older. These are all excellent reasons why someone might decide a one-fund portfolio is right for them.

What are the cons of a one-fund portfolio? One is the need for more flexibility in the choice of investments. Over time, a target date fund may grow too conservative for your tastes. Vanguard LifeStrategy® is a fund of funds. You could invest in four funds separately: stocks and bonds in both US and foreign markets. What if you do not want international bonds in your portfolio? What if the percentage of stocks invested in foreign companies is more than you would like to have? If you invested in the four underlying mutual funds, you could adjust the percentage of the portfolio invested in foreign stocks or bonds to your liking. If you had different types of accounts, you could place the bonds in traditional IRAs and traditional workplace retirement accounts and improve tax efficiency. Finally, the expense ratio will be slightly higher for an all-in-one fund than if you invested in several low-cost index funds that give approximately the same overall asset allocation.

This type of analysis can evaluate other straightforward portfolios that include multiple funds. One example would be the classic three-fund portfolio (total US stock market, total international stock market, total US bond market). For example, one might consider adding REITs or a small-cap value index fund to a three-fund portfolio. Do you add one or both funds? Are there any other options? What are the perceived benefits of adding these funds to a three-fund portfolio? If there are benefits, what are the drawbacks? Would the added complexity of the portfolio create more concerns about behavioral biases? Would adding these funds increase the expense ratio for the portfolio? Although some questions may not have clear-cut answers, they are essential to consider when determining the complexity of your portfolio. Your best portfolio may have a lower expected return. The value of simplicity may be difficult to quantify.

Investment Expenses

Cost is a factor when selecting the investments to place in our portfolio. Low-cost index funds track the US stock market, total international stock market, total US bond market, and other broad ranges of securities. Fidelity even has some at no cost: the Fidelity° Zero funds. All else being equal, a lower expense ratio is better. But don't let expenses be the only factor you consider. It is essential to feel comfortable with your investments and portfolio. Most people will probably not view an overall portfolio expense ratio of 0.07% vs. 0.09% as making a significant difference in your portfolio balances.

In Chapter 5, I included an example to illustrate the potential impact of a typical 1% AUM fee a financial advisor charges. In that example, the fee reduced the balance available at the end of accumulation by up to 25%, depending on the age at which the individual hired the financial advisor. The advisor would continue to deduct 1% of the assets under management each year, further affecting the portfolio during withdrawals. If using the 4% rule for withdrawals, in the first year, the owner would get 3% of the AUM for their living expenses, and the advisor would get 1%, or 25%, of the money withdrawn.

Later, we will discuss the pros and cons of financial advice. Note the impact advisor fees may have on your portfolio. Some choose to avoid these fees by managing their portfolio themselves. Another approach is finding the best price for the desired services. This might entail hiring a financial advisor who charges a lower-than-average AUM fee or an advice-only advisor who charges by the hour or a flat fee.

CHAPTER 8

—

Preparing Ahead for the Withdrawal Phase

MOVING FROM ACCUMULATION to withdrawal can be a significant psychological challenge, sometimes causing a loss of self-worth, boredom, and depression. Budgets may be very different in retirement as well. To transition, be deliberate with your heart, mind, and finances. In this chapter, we will discuss two areas of preparation: revisiting your non-financial game plan and budgeting for retirement. One crucial and complex retirement expense is health care. Chapter 9 is devoted to retiree health care and piecing together a retirement budget. In chapters 10 and 11, we will continue discussing strategies for withdrawal, claiming Social Security, and how to measure financial readiness for retirement.

The Non-Financial Game Plan Revisited

In the later portion of the accumulation phase, it is wise to expect and plan for foreseeable changes. In Chapter 1, we discussed the importance of having a personal non-financial plan. If you plan to retire fully after the accumulation phase, you'll have more time to allocate. If you created a personal non-financial game plan but have not reviewed it lately, it may be prudent to revisit it now.

Changes in Your Plan

Your plans may be different since you last considered them. Your interests or abilities may have changed. An aging parent with growing needs may cause you to reevaluate how you wish to spend your time and perhaps where you want to live. Maybe spending lots of time with your grandkids was part of your plan. If so, talk to your kids to make sure you agree.

You and Your Spouse

If married or committed, prioritize alignment with your significant other. Has their personal game plan changed? Should you revise any previous expectations? It is OK to have some different goals and interests; you don't have to do everything together. The issue is whether a workable joint plan will allow you to pursue personal interests while maintaining sufficient activities you wish to enjoy together.

Relocation

Are you considering relocation? Some retirees move to a favorite vacation spot but realize the novelty fades in their everyday lives. Have you considered a long-term rental to feel more confident about your decision? If relocation involves moving away from family, have you considered the impact on both yourself and your family?

Finding Meaning and Purpose

Many retire with a bucket list filled with travel destinations and enjoyable activities. Perhaps the daily grind exhausted them, and they focused on what they could look forward to in retirement. Expecting enjoyable retirement activities is fine, but solely concentrating on them can cause emptiness. Some people do not realize how much they tie their self-worth to the answer to "What do you do?" during their working years. Have you considered it? If it has played a prominent role, how do you plan to fill that void in retirement? Perhaps you can consider working part-time, volunteering, or employing your skills and talents in an area of interest. Have you thought about acquiring skills to impact others? Can you dedicate time to a cause you are passionate about, resulting in personal satisfaction?

Staying Intellectually Stimulated

Acquiring knowledge can broaden the range of activities you desire to engage in during retirement and may fend off boredom. Have you thought about a subject you'd like to delve deeper into? Have any new areas of intrigue emerged in recent years? Perhaps learning more about them or a vacation in New Zealand belongs on that bucket list. Yes, experiencing the Great Walks of New Zealand is high on my bucket list.

The Changing Budget in Retirement

First comes the non-financial plan, then the budget; you must know what you want in retirement before creating a budget. You may ask, *But how will my current budget change in retirement? Is there a simple way to estimate my retirement budget based on my current pre-retirement budget? Experts say that most people will need less than their current income in retirement. How much is the reduction?* Some simple rules of thumb suggest an 80% replacement rate but the amount you need may differ. An affluent and frugal retiree may need much less than 80% of their pre-retirement annual income during retirement. If you want and can afford expensive international travel, your replacement rate may be over 100%. But it is even more complicated than that. The replacement percentage necessary is likely to change for every year of retirement, so where do we start? Start with the expenditures most of us can expect as we age.

Average Consumer Income and Spending by Age

The Consumer Expenditure Survey (CES) is an ongoing survey that measures consumer spending in the United States for broad categories such as food, housing, apparel and services, transportation, health care, and entertainment. The US Bureau of Labor Statistics publishes tabulated data for various population subgroups. The data below, from the 2020–2021 CES, focuses on two-person consumer units by the age of the reference person. Here is a summarized portion of Table 3620 of the publication.[15]

Table 8.1 Consumer Expenditures in the US, 2021-2022
Two-Person Consumer Units By Age

	Age 55-64	Age 65-74	Age 75+
Income before taxes	114,861	82,896	62,469
Income after taxes	97,244	71,072	61,173
Earners	1.3	0.7	0.3
Food at home	5,998	5,656	5,548
Food away from home	3,543	3,129	2,364
Shelter	14,188	12,847	10,907
Household furnishings and equipment	3,307	3,449	2,369
Apparel and services	1,590	1,460	986
Transportation	13,156	11,028	8,012
Health care	7,254	8,959	9,405
Entertainment	4,411	4,545	2,775

Table 8.1 shows that from age 55 onward, the average two-person household has less income but spends less and pays less in taxes as they age. The results also reveal that although after-tax income in the 65 to 74 age bracket is about 27% less than that of the 55 to 64 age bracket, the older age group spends more on household furnishings, household equipment, and entertainment than their more youthful counterparts. Both categories see large drops in expenditures by those over 75. For the oldest cohort, expenses are lowest across the board, with one exception: health care. On average, the cost of health care increased with age while after-tax income decreased. In the 55 to 64

---

15   https://www.bls.gov/cex/tables/cross-tab/mean/cu-size-by-age-2-persons-2021-2022.pdf

age bracket, health care expenditures were about 7.5% of after-tax income; for those 75 and older, it was about 15.4%.

Potential Areas of Budgetary Changes in Retirement

Earlier, we mentioned the 4% rule. Someone adhering to this rule of thumb would withdraw 4% of their assets in year number one of retirement and then increase that figure each year for inflation. Future expenses generally don't rise with inflation, but some, such as health care, grow faster than general inflation and become a more significant portion of income. Others decrease with age. Following are several expenses that could change during retirement.

Vacation

Retirement years are often categorized into three stages: go-go, slow-go, and no-go. As we age, both our general health and physical abilities decrease. Vacation budgets usually decrease with age during withdrawal, although each situation is unique. Consider the vacations on your bucket list that you would like to take while in retirement, especially relatively expensive ones. What level of physical ability do they require? Would you benefit more from these vacations early in retirement when you expect better health? You may also want to consider the older people in your family, like your parents, aunts, and uncles. When did they slow down? None of us knows when or to what extent our health will decline, but few retirees expect extensive travel after turning 80. Estimating vacation spending decline in retirement is imprecise, but it won't increase with inflation each year. You may wish to estimate when these three stages of retirement will occur for you and figure out a vacation budget for each period. You can always revise your lifetime retirement budget as your situation changes.

Housing

Are you bringing a mortgage into retirement that you will pay off during your life? If so, principal and interest payments will disappear at some point. Unlike other expenses, these payments won't inflate with a fixed mortgage. If you will have a mortgage in retirement, consider both factors.

Another consideration is any expected change in housing. If you want to purchase a vacation home, estimate when and figure costs into your retirement budget, including related expenses for new household furnishings and equipment. If you are downsizing, consider any estimated cost savings, including lower property taxes. You could add any net proceeds to your investment portfolio.

Have you thought about changing your primary state of residence? There are many non-financial reasons someone may wish to move to another state, such as a better climate and being closer to family. While those reasons may be more influential than any financial reasons, know that they can affect your financial plan. Below are some financial considerations if you are contemplating changing your primary state of residence.

- ➤ Cost of living
- ➤ Real estate costs
- ➤ State income tax rate
- ➤ Property taxes
- ➤ Taxation of Social Security benefits
- ➤ Taxation of pensions and other retirement income sources

➜ State and local sales taxes
➜ State estate and inheritance taxes

From a financial perspective, the eight factors mentioned above would most likely affect your unique situation. States all collect revenue; they do it in different ways. Think about what you have accumulated in your investment accounts, the relative amounts in each type of account, how you spend your discretionary income, the size of your current or expected Social Security benefit, and the value of the house you live in or plan to live in. These can all affect your total state taxes. Some states have no income taxes, but that does not mean it is the lowest-cost state for you. People consider Tennessee a tax-friendly state because it has no income tax, but according to the Tax Foundation, Tennessee recently had the country's highest combined state and average local sales tax rate.[16] The point is not to focus on one factor when making a big decision like this.

Of course, this information helps you understand state taxes, even if you do not move to another state. The Tax Foundation has additional information on taxation for each state. Another online resource is State-by-State Guide to Taxes on Retirees, published by Kiplinger.[17]

Federal income taxes

What is the situation with federal income taxes? For high-wage earners in the United States, most income after a standard or itemized deduction is typically subject to federal taxes, but they have some

16   State and Local Sales Tax Rates, Midyear 2023 | Tax Foundation. https://taxfoundation.org/data/all/state/2023-sales-tax-rates-midyear/

17   State-by-State Guide to Taxes on Retirees. https://www.kiplinger.com/retirement/600892/state-by-state-guide-to-taxes-on-retirees

control over taxes in their working years. For example, they could contribute to a company 401(k) plan to reduce their taxable income in the current year but must take income in the year they earn it and pay the appropriate federal income taxes. In retirement, individuals may find opportunities to exercise greater control over taxes, such as regarding timing and, to some extent, the overall amount paid throughout their lifetime. Below are some essential distinctions between the accumulation and withdrawal stages that can affect federal taxes.

Potential Ability to Delay "Forced Income" in Retirement

In the withdrawal stage, there are often two primary sources of "forced income" for people with significant investment assets. One is required minimum distributions (RMDs). The SECURE 2.0 Act increased the age at which RMDs must be taken; it is now age 73. If you reach age 72 in 2023, the required beginning date for your first RMD is April 1, 2025 for the calendar year 2024 (when you reach age 73). RMDs apply to workplace retirement plans, such as 401(k) plans, and individual retirement accounts, including traditional IRAs, Sep IRAs, and SIMPLE IRAs.[18]

The other primary source is Social Security. Some people believe you must claim Social Security benefits when you stop working but this is not the case. Earned Social Security benefits can be claimed anytime between the ages of 62 and 70. For most Americans, Social Security is their most significant source of retirement income and can be a crucial portion of it, even for many affluent people. Usually, it is also the only retirement resource that is indexed to inflation. For

18   For more information, see Retirement Plan and IRA Required Minimum Distributions FAQs | Internal Revenue Service. https://www.irs.gov/retirement-plans/retirement-plan-and-ira-required-minimum-distributions-faqs

all these reasons, Social Security is a precious asset to optimize in retirement planning.

The typical American retires in their early 60s, but neither RMDs nor Social Security needs to be taken before age 70. This gives a potential window with no forced income from these two sources. The lack of significant forced income sources allows flexibility in withdrawal amounts and sources. Chapter 10 discusses Social Security and how to use this asset in a retirement cash-flow plan.

Potentially More Control Over the Current Effective Average Tax Rate in Retirement

In our working years, most of our income usually comes from wages. In retirement, several potential sources may be available for income each year but are subject to different tax rates. Qualified distributions from a Roth IRA or Roth 401(k) are tax-free. The federal tax rate for qualified dividends and long-term capital gains from sales in a taxable brokerage account can be as low as 0%. The tax rate is 0%, 15%, or 20%, depending on filing status and total taxable income. Interest payments, non-qualified dividends, wages from part-time jobs, or distributions from sources such as a traditional IRA or 401(k) are all taxed as ordinary income. Social Security payments add another level of complexity once they begin. Their taxation differs from the assets mentioned above and can increase taxes paid for the withdrawal of other investment assets!

Sound complicated? It can be challenging to figure out the most effective retirement withdrawal strategy. The plan entails calculating yearly withdrawals from every source. Additionally, it involves determining the optimal time to claim Social Security based on your prominent financial objectives. Thankfully, financial planning software helps make the task more manageable and can be a valuable exercise. Flexibility regarding the amount and source of withdrawals can also offer the option to decide when to pay taxes—now or later.

Consider the following example. Dave is single and planning to retire in a few months at age 62. Until he turned 55, all his investments were in his employer-sponsored 401(k) plan and a traditional IRA. When he turned 55, he increased his retirement savings rate. He contributed the maximum allowed into his 401(k) and IRA and invested his increased savings in a taxable brokerage account. His account balances are $900,000 in the traditional 401(k), $200,000 in his traditional IRA, and $250,000 in his taxable brokerage account. Because all his contributions to his brokerage account were over the last seven years, most of the money came from his contributions. He contributed $200,000 and has $50,000 in unrealized capital gains. He receives about $5,000 in qualified dividends from the stocks invested in the brokerage account. When he retires, he will roll his 401(k) over into his IRA for an expected combined balance of about $1,100,000. He has no other expected income as he plans to delay taking Social Security benefits to age 70.

In this example, Dave's only forced income is about $5,000 in qualified dividends. He wishes to live on $80,000 after federal taxes in the upcoming year. Dave could pull money from his IRA or brokerage account for an additional $75,000 in income, plus any taxes that need to be paid. If he pulled all $75,000 from the brokerage account, he would only report the portions that were capital gains. Dave's brokerage account balance includes 80% contributions and

20% investment gains. If all the withdrawals were long-term capital gains and he used an average cost basis method, he would have 20% of $75,000—or $15,000—in long-term capital gains. His total income would be $20,000. In 2024, the 0% tax bracket for long-term capital gains and qualified dividends for single filers went up to $47,025, so no federal taxes would need to be paid. Could Dave do something else and remain in the 0% tax bracket? He probably has better options. He could withdraw some money from his traditional IRA and take the remaining money from his taxable account while remaining in the 0% tax bracket. If the opportunity presents itself, it is often a good idea to generate ordinary income in the zero percent tax bracket.

Dave could also withdraw more money from his traditional IRA and pay some taxes. Why pay more taxes than necessary? Sometimes, doing so now prevents a larger tax bill in the future. The goal of tax management in retirement is not to pay the least tax for the current tax year; a holistic plan minimizing the impact of lifetime taxes is a better goal.

* * *

Another thought occupies Dave's mind. If he retires as planned when he turns 62, he will need to purchase health coverage until age 65 when he is eligible for Medicare. He could receive a premium tax credit, depending on his income. In the next chapter, we will discuss retiree health coverage in the United States before and after eligibility for Medicare.

CHAPTER 9

—

Health Care and the Retirement Budget

IN THE LAST chapter, we discussed updating a personal game plan and budgeting for retirement. One portion of the budget a retiree has yet to address is health care. The cost of health care in retirement is a significant concern for most Americans. Since knowing and budgeting for suitable care can pose challenges, the first part of this chapter examines those options and concludes with assembling a retirement budget.

Planning for Retiree Health Care Costs

Health care costs for retirees in the United States can be classified into three categories:

1. If retiring before age 65, the cost of health coverage before Medicare is a concern.
2. Retiring at age 65, health care costs while on Medicare must be considered.
3. Long-term care provided by Medicare is minimal and needs a separate examination.

Health Care Before Age 65

Most retirees in the United States are not fortunate enough to have earned lifetime health benefits from their former employers. Are you retiring before 65? You may wish to consider COBRA for continued coverage of up to 18 months, but that can be expensive. COBRA charges the full price for your health coverage, plus your former employer may add up to a 2% administration fee. Many do not realize what their employer pays toward their monthly cost of health coverage premiums. According to the "Employer Health Benefits 2023 Annual Survey" published by the Kaiser Family Foundation, the average cost for family coverage was $23,968 in 2023; an average of $6,575 was paid by the employee and $17,393 was paid by the employer.[19] For single coverage, the figures were $8,435, with employees paying an average of $1,401 and employers paying the remaining $7,034. The value of employer-provided health coverage may also be stated on your W-2 form in Box 12DD and includes what you and your employer collectively paid toward the monthly premiums.

One option that may cost considerably less is purchasing health coverage in your state's marketplace. Substantial premium tax credits may be available, depending on your income. "Income" here is defined

19   https://files.kff.org/attachment/Employer-Health-Benefits-Survey-2023-Annual-Survey-Sum-mary-of-Findings.pdf

as your modified adjusted gross income (MAGI); the adjusted gross income that would appear on your federal tax return plus any untaxed foreign income, non-taxable Social Security benefits, and tax-exempt interest, such as interest on municipal bonds. Notice the list of adjustments includes non-taxable Social Security benefits. The total gross value of Social Security counts toward MAGI, even if some or all of it is exempt from federal income taxes. By claiming Social Security before reaching the age of 65, the expense of health coverage could rise if that coverage is acquired through your state's marketplace. Choosing the most suitable date to claim Social Security is a reason for reflection, encompassing factors that may go unnoticed by some. Social Security is discussed more in the next chapter.

Monthly costs for premiums, after-tax credit, and maximum out-of-pocket costs are based on income relative to the poverty level for your family size. The federal poverty level for individuals in 2024 was $15,060, while for a household of two, it was $20,440.[20] Information on costs for premiums, premium tax credits (subsidies), and out-of-pocket maximum expenses per year can be found with an online calculator provided by the Kaiser Family Foundation (Health Insurance Marketplace Calculator). The calculator provides data for the US average and costs based on state, county, and zip code. Table 9.1 was generated from this calculator and assumes coverage was unavailable from your or your spouse's employer, there are no children 20 or younger enrolling, and no one enrolling used tobacco.

20   Poverty Guidelines | ASPE. https://aspe.hhs.gov/topics/poverty-economic-mobility/
        poverty-guidelines

Table 9.1 2024 National Average Health Insurance Marketplace Costs and Estimated Premium Tax Credits, Age 62, Silver Plans

	One Person Household			Two Person Household		
% Poverty	Annual Cost	Tax Credit	OOP Limit	Annual Cost	Tax Credit	OOP Limit
150%	$0	$12,866	$3,150	$0	$25,731	$6,300
200%	$583	$12,282	$3,150	$789	$24,942	$6,300
201%	$598	$12,268	$7,550	$809	$24,923	$15,100
250%	$1,458	$11,408	$7,550	$1,972	$23,759	$15,100
251%	$1,478	$11,387	$9,450	$1,978	$23,731	$18,900
300%	$2,624	$10,241	$9,450	$3,550	$22,182	$18,900
350%	$3,700	$9,166	$9,450	$5,004	$20,727	$18,900
400%	$4,957	$7,908	$9,450	$6,705	$19,026	$18,900

Source:
https://www.kff.org/interactive/subsidy-calculator

Let's begin by examining the numbers for individuals living alone. The costs for a health coverage silver plan are $0 for MAGI equal to 150% of the poverty level ($22,590 in 2024), with a maximum out-of-pocket expense of $3,150 and a subsidy valued at $12,866. As a person's MAGI grows and exceeds 150% of the poverty level, the subsidy decreases and increases the annual premium paid. With a MAGI equal to 200% of the poverty level ($30,120 in 2024), the yearly premium increases but is only $583 per year or about $49 per month, and the out-of-pocket maximum remains $3,150. What happens as modified AGI increases from 200% to 201% of the poverty level? The annual premium would rise modestly to $598 from $583, but the out-of-pocket maximum would surge from $3,150 to $7,550—an increase of almost 240%. Surpassing the 200% limit could result in $4,400 in added expenses in 2024. Another change in the out-of-pocket maximum happens when MAGI increases from 250% to 251% of the poverty level—it jumps again by about 25% from $7,550 to $9,450. The same increase occurs for two-person households; the amounts are just twice as large. The out-of-pocket maximum increases from $6,300 to $15,100 as MAGI increases from 200% to 201% of the poverty line, and it increases from $15,100 to $18,900 as MAGI increases from 250% to 251% of the poverty line.

Now, let's return to Dave's situation mentioned in the previous chapter. Recall that he wishes to live on $80,000 yearly after federal income taxes. His assets included a brokerage account with $250,000, 80% or $200,000 of his contributions, and the remaining 20%, or $50,000, in unrealized capital gains. Dave has significant medical issues and would like to limit his out-of-pocket costs to a maximum of $3,150 per year. Dave's qualified dividends have been around $5,000 but fluctuate yearly, so he does not want to shoot for precisely a MAGI equal to $30,120 (200% of the poverty line) to reach his goal. He decides an estimated MAGI of $29,500 is a suitable target for him. Dave knows his MAGI could be close to $20,000 ($5,000 in qualified dividends plus 80% of $75,000) if he pulled all the money he needed from his brokerage account because 80% was his contribution and would not be subject to taxes. His goal is workable. He estimates the combination of traditional IRA and brokerage account withdrawals to produce an estimated MAGI close to $29,500. Why does he take any money out of his traditional IRA? Dave realizes he is in a lower tax bracket than he will probably be in the future, so he wants to take as much out of his traditional IRA as possible without losing his low out-of-pocket maximum for health care. As the year progresses, he monitors his average cost basis and dividends from his taxable brokerage account and makes any necessary adjustments to his withdrawal strategy.

You might recall Dave's plans to delay claiming Social Security to age 70. What if he claimed his benefit before reaching the age of

70? Suppose Dave could receive $2,000 monthly at age 62 in Social Security benefits. Dave's MAGI would include both taxable and non-taxable Social Security benefits. If he collected Social Security for a full calendar year, his MAGI would be $24,000 in Social Security benefits and about $5,000 in qualified dividends. That is already a MAGI of $29,000 before withdrawing money from his IRA and brokerage account to cover the additional $51,000 in living expenses plus any federal taxes owed. In this situation, Dave could not keep his MAGI under $30,120 while receiving the desired income. The presence of Social Security income would have diminished the flexibility he possessed in his withdrawal strategy.

Health Care Starting at Age 65

President Lyndon Johnson signed Medicare into law on July 30, 1965, with enrollment beginning the following day. It initially consisted of two components: Medicare Part A and Medicare Part B. President George W. Bush signed the Medicare Prescription Drug, Improvement, and Modernization Act of 2003 to establish prescription drug coverage. Because of this Act, Medicare Part D, covering prescription drugs, went into effect on January 1, 2006. This Act also did two crucial things: It established the modern Medicare Advantage (Medicare Part C) program and adjusted premiums based on income. Understanding Medicare, Parts A, B, C, and D, and Medigap (Medicare Supplemental Insurance) plans is vital to choosing the right health coverage when you are approaching age 65. We begin our overview of Medicare by discussing eligibility for benefits and some Medicare terminology. After that, we will summarize some key points about Medicare Parts A through D and Medigap policies.

Original Medicare (Part A and Part B)

A person is eligible for Medicare if they are at least 65 years old and would qualify for Social Security or railroad retirement benefits. A person at least 65 qualifies for Social Security benefits if they have earned at least 40 quarters of credit. A maximum of four quarters of coverage can be earned in a year. In 2024, $1,730 in earnings subject to Social Security taxation earned one credit. Four quarters of credit could be earned with a wage of at least $6,920 per year. In prior years, the earnings needed to earn a credit were lower; in 1978, the amount required for one credit was $250. Each year since then, it has been adjusted for national average wage growth.[21] If you have at least 10 years of Social Security-covered earnings where your wages were at least the minimum amount needed to earn four credits, you have earned a right to Medicare benefits starting at age 65. A person under the age of 65 may qualify if they are on Social Security disability, have ALS, or have end-stage renal disease.[22]

Costs for medical care under Medicare may come from monthly premiums, copayments, and coinsurance. Copayments are a fixed cost and copayments are a percentage of costs. For example, under Medicare Part A, days 21 through 100 spent in a skilled nursing facility required a $204 copayment per day in 2024. Under Medicare Part B, the 2024 coinsurance amount for Medicare-approved costs for durable medical equipment like wheelchairs and walkers was 20%. Some are unfamiliar with Original Medicare terminology, including

21   Quarter of Coverage. ssa.gov

22   Who's Eligible for Medicare? https://www.hhs.gov/answers/medicare-and-medicaid/who-is-eligible-for-medicare/index.html

the definition of a "benefit period." Here is a description of the term from Medicare's glossary:[23]

> **Benefit period:** The way Original Medicare measures your use of hospital and skilled nursing facility (SNF) services. A benefit period begins the day you're admitted as an inpatient in a hospital or SNF. The benefit period ends when you have received no inpatient hospital care (or skilled care in an SNF) for 60 days. A new benefit period begins if you enter a hospital or SNF after one benefit period ends. You must pay the inpatient hospital deductible for each benefit period. There's no limit to the number of benefit periods.

Medicare Part A, hospital insurance, generally has no monthly premium. If you don't qualify for Medicare, you may be able to purchase coverage, but it is not cheap. In 2024, the cost to buy coverage was $278 or $505 per month, depending on how long you or your spouse worked and paid Medicare taxes. The deductible in 2024 was also $1,632 per benefit period, not per year. Remember, there can be more than one benefit period per year, each with a $1,632 deductible.[24]

Medicare Part B covers physician visits, necessary outpatient expenses, and preventive care. Visits to the emergency room are covered under Part B, not Part A. The premium was at least $174.70 monthly in 2024, with a $240 deductible. The premium is based on income two years prior unless you had a life-changing event that reduced your income level. So, typically, the premiums paid in

---

23   Glossary | Medicare. https://www.medicare.gov/glossary/b

24   See Costs | Medicare for more details on costs for Medicare Parts A through D. https://www.medicare.gov/basics/costs/medicare-costs

2024 would be based on income in 2022. The table below summarizes the 2024 monthly Medicare Part B coverage premium based on MAGI.

Table 9.2 2024 Medicare Part B Premiums by 2022 MAGI and Filing Status

Individual	Married Filing Joint	Married Filing Separate	Premium
$103,000 or less	$206,000 or less	$103,000 or less	$174.70
Above $103,000 up to $129,000	Above $206,000 up to $258,000	Not Applicable	$244.60
Above $129,000 up to $161,000	Above $258,000 up to $322,000	Not Applicable	$349.40
Above $161,000 up to $193,000	Above $322,000 up to $386,000	Not Applicable	$454.20
Above $193,000 and less than $500,000	Above $386,000 and less than $750,000	Above $103,000 and less than $397,000	$559.00
$500,000 or above	$750,000 or above	$397,000 and above	$594.00

Source:
https://www.medicare.gov/basics/costs/medicare-costs

Note that the premiums have a characteristic like the marketplace out-of-pocket maximums: If you go just slightly over the MAGI bracket for your filing status, it can cause a significant increase in cost. The extra cost for a monthly premium because of higher income is called the income-related monthly adjustment amount, or IRMAA. Examine the 2024 Medicare Part B premium for a person with a $103,000 MAGI in 2022. They would pay $174.70 per month in Medicare Part B premiums. If they were covered for the entire year, that would amount to $2,096.40. If the MAGI bracket is exceeded by $500, it leads to an $838.80 increase in the annual Medicare Part

B premium. If you consider the additional fee a tax, your effective tax rate on that last $500 in earned income would be over 100%! It might cause one to yell, "IRMAA!" When planning for health coverage costs, know how your prior tax returns might affect your Medicare costs in the future. If you expect to be close to the upper end of a MAGI income bracket for IRMAA fees, see if you can lower your MAGI by altering your withdrawal strategy. Some forward-looking financial planning software will consider IRMAA fees, like New Retirement, as previously mentioned.

Original Medicare and Medicare parts A and B cover various medical needs. However, there are some things that neither Part A nor Part B cover: Eyeglasses, hearing aids, prescription drugs, and the cost of nursing homes. It sounds to me like a laundry list of medical coverage people over 65 may need! Fortunately, there are several options to get additional coverage. These include Medicare Part D, Medigap plans, Medicare Part C, and long-term care insurance. Below, I summarize information about Medicare parts C and D in addition to Medigap plans. After that, we will explore strategies for managing the cost of long-term care that could impact your retirement budget.

Medigap Plans

The gaps in health coverage not covered by Medicare Part A and Part B are often referred to as Medicare gaps. Those gaps include:

- Deductibles for Part A and Part B
- Copayments for extended hospitalization under Part A
- Coinsurance under Part B
- Costs exceeding Part B approved charges
- Most self-administered prescription drugs

➤ Skilled nursing facility care coinsurance

Standardized Medicare supplement plans, called Medigap plans, are available from private vendors and address at least some gaps. There are 10 standardized plans: A, B, C, D, F, G, K, L, M, and N. Plans F and G offer a high-deductible version and have the highest enrollment nationwide. As of 2021, over 70% of those enrolled in a Medigap plan were enrolled in either Plan F or Plan G according to "The State of Medicare Supplement Coverage" published by America's Health Insurance Plans in 2023. While Plan F had the highest enrollment in 2021, its popularity diminished between 2018 and 2021. Meanwhile, enrollment in Plan G nearly doubled.[25] What do these two plans have in common? Of the 10 plans, they are the only ones that cover excess charges of Part B. Appendix A summarizes the gap coverage for each of the 10 standardized plans in the publication.

Here are some critical points about the new Medigap plans:

➤ Does not include coverage for prescription drugs
➤ Typically does not provide dental, vision, or hearing aid coverage
➤ Limited long-term care benefits

You must look elsewhere for insurance coverage for some of these needs.

To enroll in a Medigap plan, you must already be enrolled in Medicare Part A and Part B. Filing for Medicare Part B starts a six-month open enrollment window in which you cannot be denied coverage or

25   See Table 4. https://www.ahip.org/documents/202301-AHIP_MedicareSuppCvg-v03.pdf

experience rate increases because of a pre-existing condition. If you file after that, you may be subject to medical underwriting.

What if you are still working past the age of 65? You should file for Medicare Part A as you approach age 65 if you qualify for it. It is free. However, you can delay filing for Medicare Part B until you are no longer covered under your employer's health coverage plan. If you filed for Medicare Part A and Part B at age 65, continued working until age 66, and then developed an unexpected health condition, you might be subject to Medigap underwriting.

Medicare Part D

As mentioned above, newly issued Medigap plans cannot include prescription drug coverage, so many people also buy Medicare Part D. The monthly premium for Medicare Part D is the premium your plan charges plus any IRMAA fees. Table 9.2 shows the IRMAA fees for Medicare Part B coverage; the IRMAA fees for Medicare Part D are based on the same income brackets. In 2024, these fees added anywhere from $12.90 to $81 a month to premiums.[26]

Coverage and cost are the two main things to consider when comparing Medicare Part D plans; check to see whether the prescription drugs you currently take are covered under each program. Depending on medication costs, paying a more significant premium for enhanced benefits may be wise.

Medicare Advantage (Medicare Part C)

Medicare Part C is an alternative to enrolling in a Medigap plan. It is desirable for those wishing to have low monthly premiums and

26   Monthly premium for drug plans | Medicare. https://www.medicare.gov/drug-coverage-part-d/costs-for-medicare-drug-coverage/monthly-premium-for-drug-plans

often provides benefits not covered in Medicare parts A and B, such as vision and dental care and hearing exams. It also includes prescription drug coverage, so people with a Medicare Advantage plan do not need to purchase Medicare Part D. Certain plans even come with a $0 premium. As a result, some people covered by Medicare Part C only pay one premium—their Medicare Part B premium. Expanded coverage with no increase in premiums sounds nice on the surface, but there are reasons people sign up for Medigap plans and Medicare Part D instead of Medicare Part C. One reason is that the cost can be significantly higher when care is needed under Medicare Part C due to deductibles, coinsurance, and maximum out-of-pocket limits. Also, the beneficiary must live in a geographic area where the plan accepts enrollees; not everyone has the option of enrolling in Medicare Part C.[27]

Long-Term Care Costs

Long-term care is a potentially massive expense in retirement, and surrounded by lots of uncertainty. Let's start by examining what constitutes long-term care, its cost, and how often people need it. We will then discuss how a retirement budget can address this care.

Most long-term care is not medical care. Instead, it helps with the activities of daily living (ADLs) that one must be able to perform to live independently. Insurance companies typically consider six ADLs to determine if a person qualifies for long-term care benefits: bathing, eating, dressing, ability to transfer, toileting, and continence. If someone requires assistance with multiple ADLs, they typically meet the criteria for long-term care benefits.

---

27   For more information, visit www.medicare.gov.

The help needed will vary depending on physical and cognitive functioning levels. Some individuals with declining physical abilities may need a few hours of daily help but can still perform many tasks independently. Those with cognitive issues may primarily need supervision. Some require assistance for almost every ADL. Care is provided in different settings, and the cost depends on the level and type of need.

The 2021 Genworth Cost of Care Survey provides national and state-specific estimates for care costs.[28] The results show the national average fee of $26 per hour for homemaker services, $27 per hour for a home health aide, and $78 per day for adult day care. Assisted living with a private room costs $54,000 annually. As expected, nursing home facilities were the most expensive, at $94,000 per year for semi-private rooms and $108,405 for private rooms.

How frequently do individuals require long-term care? Long-TermCare.gov says that around 70% of 65-year-old individuals require long-term care in their lifetime.[29] On average, care lasts three years; two at home and one in a facility. Most home care is often unpaid and provided by family and friends. Women require approximately 68% more years of care than men, on average; women receive an average of 3.7 years of care, while men receive 2.2 years. Most people will need long-term care sometime in their life, and we have seen how expensive it is. Medicare potentially only provides limited short-term help for long-term care needs, so funding must come from somewhere else. Here are six ways to cover long-term care costs:

28   Genworth Cost of Care Survey. https://pro.genworth.com/riiproweb/productinfo/pdf/282102.pdf

29   How Much Care Will You Need? | ACL Administration for Community Living. LongTermCare.gov

1. **Self-insure.** This option is solely for those who are financially well-off.

2. **Medicaid.** Medicaid covers long-term care, but you must have little financially. Medicaid's care quality and availability of facilities and doctors may be limited, but it might be the sole practical choice for many people.

3. **Life insurance.** Life Insurance may provide options to pay for long-term care needs through loans, hybrid policies of long-term care and life insurance, and long-term care riders added to a life insurance policy. Life settlements also allow someone to sell their policy for its present value.

4. **Annuities.** Annuities can be created with a long-term care benefit rider. Another type of annuity, not specifically designed for long-term care, may also be worth consideration: A qualified longevity annuity contract (QLAC) is a deferred, fixed-annuity contract purchased with money from a qualified retirement account, such as a traditional 401(k) or traditional IRA. The maximum purchase price for a QLAC is $200,000 per person, not per retirement account. Payments may be deferred up to age 85. QLACs can provide large monthly payments for people worried about outliving their money, but the downside is lowering your estate's value if you pass away before the payments start or shortly after they begin.

5. **Home equity.** A reverse mortgage can provide income for long-term care needs like in-home care or facility care when the first spouse needs it. This income stream stops once the second spouse no longer lives in the home. A homeowner living alone could also sell their house to help pay for facility care.

6. **Long-term care insurance.** I saved the most obvious for last. Long-term care insurance is notoriously expensive and premiums continue to rise. Because of the high cost and potential of not needing long-term care, many are reluctant to purchase it and investigate other options.

Our cost for medical care after age 65 admittedly involves considerable uncertainty. I believe few would argue with me when I say it is typically the most challenging part of estimating a retirement budget. That said, a reasonable retirement budget should consider an estimate of medical costs. Start with your current or expected medical needs to see which types of coverage appear to make the most sense. It might also be wise to build an escalation for out-of-pocket costs with age since that typically happens.

Another area of uncertainty is taxes. Significant changes to tax laws in the future could certainly affect your budget. Remember, estimates are just that: *estimates*. Things can change. Your or your spouse's health might change, affecting medical costs and planned travel. Tax rates may change. You can always change your plan as new information becomes available and do stress tests to see how your portfolio might perform under various "what if" scenarios. One possible approach is to assess your current situation and costs in today's dollars. Additionally, you could consider utilizing statistics such as the increase in medical expenses with age and the typical usage of long-term care as a general guideline.

Assembling the Retirement Budget

Creating a retirement budget involves analyzing anticipated expenses that differ based on your age and strategy. Here is a general outline of the process using an example.

Julie is approaching 62 and plans to retire fully on her birthday. She is divorced and has one child, an adult daughter, who is married with three children. Julie loves spending time with her family, especially her grandchildren, who live nearby. Julie is happily living in a two-bedroom condominium, which she recently paid off. She has no desire to move.

Julie first considers the life expectancy she wishes to assume for her retirement budget. Considering family history and US Life Tables, she makes her decision. The most recent US Life Tables is for 2021, released in November 2023.[30] Table 3 in the publication shows the average life expectancy of a 62-year-old female is 22.1 years, which takes her to age 84.1. Her relatives had above-average longevity, so she desires a plan that would likely cover her expenses to age 95, or 33 more years.

She breaks down her estimated retirement budget into six age brackets: age 62 to 65, age 65 to 70, age 70 to 80, age 80 to 90, age 90 to 92, and age 92 to 95. She expects the significant changes in expenses with age to fall into three categories. One category is labeled "get out and do stuff." This category includes expenses for vacations, entertainment, and transportation. She strongly desires to travel in the first three years of retirement to create special memories with her grandchildren while they are still young. Julie plans to be quite active

---

30   This set of tables, and others released in prior years, can be obtained at Products - Life Tables - Homepage. https://www.cdc.gov/nchs/products/life_tables.htm

for the rest of her 60s, with a slight dip in expenses in this category from age 65 to age 70. Planned expenses for this category decline again in her 70s and experience an even more significant decline in her 80s. Her assumed no-go years are in her 90s.

She budgets significant changes in expenses for health care and long-term care. Based on her situation, she estimates her health care expenses will be lowest from age 65 to 70. She builds a rough estimate for escalation in out-of-pocket medical expenses from age 70 forward, considering typical growth in expenditures by age. Health coverage costs for ages 62 to 65 are expected to be a little more than once she receives Medicare at age 65.

Julie has heard that, on average, women need 3.7 years of long-term care. She budgeted for five years of long-term care. Her budget assumes two years of home care with 20 hours a week of help, followed by three years in a skilled nursing care facility. She researches the current costs in her local area and puts them into her budget.

Julie's estimated retirement budget includes $75,000 per year from age 62 to 65, $69,000 per year from age 65 to 70, $65,000 per year in her 70s, $62,000 per year in her 80s, $95,000 per year from age 90 to 92, and $130,000 from age 92 to 95.

Later, we will continue to examine Julie's situation and the critical decision of when to claim her Social Security benefits, computing results for potential start ages between 62 and 70. Is her financial nest egg large enough that she will feel confident it will last to age 95 without significant cuts? We will discuss ways to measure retirement readiness and what options Julie might consider if she wants to enhance the longevity of her nest egg. Chapter 11 discusses drawing down your assets in different accounts subject to different tax rates and how Social Security affects an optimal cash-flow retirement plan.

CHAPTER 10

—

An Introduction to Social Security

MANY THINGS WE can control during the accumulation phase remain in our control when we withdraw our assets in retirement, such as asset allocation, location, portfolio complexity, and expenses. Even time in the market remains under our control to some extent during the withdrawal stage. We can invest for those who will inherit our estate upon our death. However, the withdrawal process presents some unique decisions not encountered during accumulation. Chapter 10 and Chapter 11 will discuss two additional choices: when to claim Social Security benefits and considerations when designing an efficient withdrawal strategy.

An Overview of the Social Security Decision

People who qualify can claim Social Security benefits as early as age 62, which provides an immediate source of income to help replace a portion of a lost paycheck. For most people, Social Security is a significant source of retirement income. However, individuals who delay taking benefits up to age 70 will see an increase in their future payments for each month of delay. Another potential reason to delay benefits is that Social Security payments are indexed to inflation. Many do not understand their options or the full implications of their decision.

When do people decide to claim their Social Security benefits? The average benefits claim age has risen in the past two decades. One reason for this trend is the change in what Social Security refers to as full retirement age (FRA). The size of one's benefit will depend on when a person claims their benefits relative to their FRA. Everyone's FRA used to be age 65. However, it is now determined by your year of birth. Anyone born before 1938 has an FRA of 65. Anyone born after 1938 has an FRA between 65 + 2 months and 67. Those born from 1943 through 1954 have an FRA of 66. Starting with the birth year of 1955, the FRA increases by two months each year until reaching 67 for the birth year 1960; anyone born then or later has a full retirement age of 67.

The annual supplement to the Social Security Bulletin contains statistical data on Social Security benefits. The 2023 publication provides data from the 2022 supplement on the benefits awarded to retired workers. Claiming age for both men and women has risen since 2005, when the average age was 63.6, with 50.2% of men and 54.3% of women claiming benefits at age 62. Those average claiming ages would be even earlier if you excluded people collecting disability benefits. These averages include conversions of disability benefits to retired worker benefits, which occur when a disabled person reaches their FRA.

Based on the data provided in the 2023 supplement, around 1,719,000 men and 1,695,000 women reported receiving benefits for the first time in 2022. The average claiming age in 2022 exceeded 65 for both men and women; it was 65.2 for men and 65.1 for women, with only 22.9% of men and 24.5% of women claiming at 62. Again, these statistics include conversions of disability benefits to retired worker benefits when the recipient reaches their FRA.

For our purposes, I wish to examine when people not previously collecting a disability benefit voluntarily claimed their retired worker benefit. I calculated the distribution for claiming age in 2022 for nondisabled retirees by excluding the 13.4% of men and 13.1% of women who had their disability benefits converted to a retired worker benefit. The results are in Table 10.1.

Table 10.1 Social Security Claiming Age in 2022 by Gender and Disability Status

Claiming Age	Men		Women	
	All	Nondisabled	All	Nondisabled
62	22.90%	26.40%	24.50%	28.20%
63	6.40%	7.40%	6.60%	7.60%
64	6.70%	7.70%	7.30%	8.40%
65 < Age < FRA	13.30%	15.40%	13.40%	15.40%
FRA (Nondisabled)	15.00%	17.30%	13.40%	15.40%
FRA (Disabled)	13.40%	NA	13.10%	NA
FRA < Age < 70	13.90%	15.90%	12.20%	14.00%
70+	8.60%	9.90%	9.50%	10.90%

Source:
2023 Annual Statistical Supplement to the Social Security Bulletin, Table 6.B5, Annual Statistical Supplement, 2023 - OASDI Benefits Awarded: Retired Workers (6.B) (ssa.gov)

About 57% of nondisabled men and 60% of nondisabled women claim their Social Security benefits before their FRA, 90% of men and 89% of women claim benefits before age 70, and about 25% delay benefits beyond their FRA.

Despite the trend toward claiming Social Security benefits later, most still choose to claim before reaching FRA. There are valid reasons for collecting early under the right circumstances. For example, a person who is not married with a short anticipated life expectancy may be wise to claim Social Security benefits at 62. However, I believe many choose to claim early despite analysis suggesting that waiting longer is probably the better financial decision. Why?

Reasons Some Choose to Claim Social Security at Age 62

Reason #1: Comfort

You work up to age 62, are accustomed to that dependable paycheck, and have contributed to an employer-sponsored 401(k) plan for years, knowing saving early and often was a good idea. Now, you stare at your 401(k) and IRA balances, questioning whether they're sufficient. Claiming Social Security at age 62 allows the continuation of a dependable "paycheck" while limiting withdrawals from your investment portfolio. This might provide a sense of comfort on the surface, but have you considered reasons to delay claiming Social Security? Is comfort driving your decision without considering other factors? Perhaps sacrificing some money for enhanced peace of mind is worth it to you, but knowing the potential cost of that comfort is wise. How much more you will receive in Social Security benefits by claiming later? There is no statement to review for that, so it's easy to overlook something when it's not visible. Have you considered whether that may cloud your judgment? Have you considered the potential increase in security you may experience in your later years, knowing that a more significant percentage of your retirement assets will be indexed to inflation? Perhaps you are valuing comfort now while downplaying the value of comfort in the future.

The last chapter ended with Julie's retirement budget. In that example, she wanted to spend extra money early in retirement for vacations with her grandchildren. Should she claim her Social Security benefit at age 62 because her need for income will be more significant early in retirement? Again, the same issues are at play. Individuals can withdraw money from retirement accounts, collect from Social Security, or do both. Make an informed decision that considers your portfolio goals and peace of mind.

Reason #2: I'll Invest Social Security Payments in the Stock Market and Be Better off

Suppose you consider claiming Social Security at age 62 and investing your monthly payments in stocks. If so, you must acknowledge that you are altering the level of risk in your portfolio. You would sell some of your future government-backed inflation-indexed payments to invest in a more volatile asset with an assumed higher expected average rate of return. Will this decision improve your situation? It depends on how you define improvement. It comes back to this fundamental question: What is the primary goal for your portfolio? Is it to maximize your estate's value when you pass away? Is it to lower the likelihood of your portfolio running out of money? Some nuances are involved here, but typically, delaying Social Security will reduce the potential ceiling of the size of your estate. If market conditions are excellent during your retirement years, this decision may be a good one in hindsight.

There is another noteworthy point to consider: If the "failure" of your portfolio is running out of money before you die, not all failures are equal. If your full retirement age is 67, delaying Social Security until 70 would increase your payment to about 177% of what you would have received at age 62. Suppose your investment portfolio drops to zero after age 70. Which Social Security payment would you prefer to accept: the one claimed at 62 or 70? The more significant benefit claimed at age 70 may at least cover your essential costs, while the reduced age 62 benefit may not.

Reason #3: Failure to Consider Survivor Benefits

One aspect of the Social Security decision involves married couples. If you are married, your age and earnings history are likely different from your spouse's. If you intend to stay together until death do you part, expected survivor benefits should be a consideration.

Dr. Paul Hemez with the US Census Bureau used data from the 2021 American Community Survey to estimate the average age difference between married couples: between opposite-sex married couples it was about 3.7 years, with larger average age differences for same-sex married couples.[31] Based on this, the following example will consider a four-year age difference between a couple. Doug, 62, is trying to decide when to claim Social Security. His wife, Courtney, is 58. Based on the 2021 US Life Tables, an average 62-year-old male has a 19.0-year life expectancy, and an average 58-year-old female

---

31   Conference Poster Template. https://www.census.gov/content/dam/Census/library/working-papers/2023/demo/sehsd-wp2023-10.pdf

has a 25.3-year life expectancy. Doug assumes he and his wife will have average life expectancies for their age and gender, Courtney will probably outlive him by an average of 6.3 years, and he knows two additional things: He has a higher earning history than his wife and thus a more considerable potential Social Security benefit. He also knows that when one spouse passes away, the surviving spouse gets to keep their own Social Security payment or receive their spouse's larger payment, but not both. By claiming Social Security later, Doug could increase Courtney's expected Social Security payments over her lifetime.

The higher wage earner is often, but not always, served best by claiming Social Security at FRA or later. Differences in life expectancy and earnings history can enhance this incentive when a spouse is likely to receive significant survivor benefits. Each situation is unique and no one should rely on generalization to decide.

Later, we will look more closely at modeling the Social Security decision for a single person like Julie, introduced in the last chapter. Examining a married couple is comparable to studying an individual but with added emphasis on survivor benefits.

Reason #4: Social Security is Going Bankrupt. Grab Your Money Now!

Fear can lead to bad financial decisions. Is worry over the uncertainty of Social Security's future warranted? Do people exaggerate it? That is for you to decide, but I have opinions on the subject. I don't have all the answers but I know where to begin. Let's start with some facts about Social Security.

The Social Security Trust Funds (SSTF), comprising the Old-Age and Survivors Insurance (OASI) Trust Fund and the Disability

Insurance (DI) Trust Fund had been increasing their asset reserves for a long time. Every year from 1982 through 2020, the asset reserves for the SSTF increased. You can review historical SSTF costs and income by year from 1957 through 2023.[32] The trust fund experienced net losses in 2021, 2022, and 2023. The shift in age demographics in the US will cause ongoing losses that will continue to grow.

In March 2023, the Social Security Administration released a report that projects trust fund depletion in 2034.[33] It also projects continuing income to cover 80% of costs up to 2097, declining to 74% in 2097. The revenue that still would come in after 2034 includes the 12.4% payroll taxes paid on wages, half paid by the employer for those not self-employed. The report also states that about 40% of people receiving Social Security pay federal income taxes on their benefits, and some of those taxes help fund the Social Security system.

Many people hear the SSTF will have a zero balance in 2034 and assume they will receive no Social Security benefit after 2034. Given the information above, this does not seem plausible. Will your benefits be reduced? It's possible, but it might not be as bad as one thinks. Various proposed solutions and their estimated impact on the Social Security funding problem have been considered, although it's uncertain which ones will come to fruition. These proposed changes could affect people differently. Some may not affect you at all.

The Committee for a Responsible Federal Budget is a nonpartisan, nonprofit organization. It has an interactive Social Security reformer

32   Trust Fund Data. https://www.ssa.gov/oact/STATS/table4a3.html

33   Summary: Actuarial Status of the Social Security Trust Funds, March 2023. https://www.ssa.gov/policy/trust-funds-summary.pdf

calculator that sheds some light on some proposed changes, including changes to the benefit formula and ways to collect more revenue.[34]

One proposed change is subjecting all wages to payroll taxes. In 2024, the 12.4% payroll tax applied only to wages up to $168,600. The employer paid half if one was not self-employed. The calculator estimates this one change would close 59% of the funding gap. This proposed change wouldn't affect you if you don't earn $168,600.

Some state and local workers are exempt from Social Security, so one proposal is to require all newly hired state and local workers to be part of the Social Security system and pay payroll taxes. This change would close about 5% of the funding gap as of this writing and would have no impact on most approaching retirement.

Let's talk about those closest to a traditional retirement age, let's call that age 55 to 62. People in that age range may have paid into the Social Security system for over three decades. Altering the rules just as they reach age 62 may seem unfair, but compare that to newcomers in the workforce. Many young people think that Social Security will not exist or will undergo considerable changes by the time they reach age 62. Specific proposals may target only those under 55 because of the fear of displeasing older voters. I don't know what changes will occur with Social Security. I fall into this age demographic so perhaps my age biases my opinion and this is wishful thinking; I do not believe that is the case but run my projections based on receiving 80% to 100% benefits using the current Social Security formula. I would feel more comfortable estimating little to no impact of Social Security changes on my future benefits the closer I was to age 62. Your perspective may differ.

---

34   The Reformer: An Interactive Tool to Fix Social Security. https://www.crfb.org/socialsecurityreformer/

How Monthly Benefits are Calculated Based on Your Earnings Record

Monthly Social Security benefits can be based on your earnings history, subject to Social Security taxes. Someone else's earnings, such as a spouse or ex-spouse, may also contribute to deriving monthly Social Security benefits. Consider the following example for Julie, who is planning retirement at age 62. The year Julie has her 62nd birthday is her eligibility year. Assume she was born in 1962, so her eligibility year is 2024. We would start with a list of her Social Security-taxed earnings by year found on her Social Security statement. Next, we adjust these earnings for average wage growth using an index. The wage index based on an eligibility year entered by the user can be found on the SSA site.[35]

Indexing applies to calendar years at least three years before the eligibility year. In this example, we adjust earnings for every year before 2022 based on the average rates of wage increases between that year and 2022. Suppose in 2007, Julie earned $56,400. The index number for that year is 1.5788732, which implies that wages increased by an average of about 57.9% between 2007 and 2022. Her 2007 indexed earnings would be $89,048. Any earnings in 2022—when Julie had her 60th birthday—or later would not be indexed for wage growth. Her actual earnings would equal her indexed earnings from 2022 forward.

The next step in the process is calculating Julie's average indexed monthly earnings (AIME). This calculation uses Julie's 35 highest indexed earnings years. The computation of AIME involves adding

35   Indexing Factors for Earnings. https://www.ssa.gov/OACT/COLA/awifactors.html

the largest 35 years of indexed earnings and dividing that figure by 420, the number of months in 35 years. In our example, Julie's AIME, based on her earnings through 2022, is assumed to be $6,551.

What would be the outcome if Julie made payments into Social Security for fewer than 35 years? First, we would need to check whether Julie qualifies for retirement benefits; someone must be fully insured to be eligible for retirement benefits by earning at least 40 credits. One can earn up to four credits in a year. For one credit in 2024, one must have $1,730 in earnings; $6,920 or more earn a maximum of four credits in 2024. If Julie accumulated at least 40 credits but possessed fewer than 35 years of earnings history, we would add all her indexed earnings and divide by 420 to calculate her AIME. If she were fully insured but had only 25 years of earnings history, the calculation of her AIME would include 10 years of zeros.

After AIME is figured, computing benefits at full retirement age is the next step. As mentioned at the outset, full retirement age is based on year of birth; anyone born between 1943 and 1954 has a full retirement age of 66. Starting with the birth year of 1955, the FRA increased by two months each year until reaching 67 for the birth year 1960. Anyone born in 1960 or later, like Julie, has a full retirement age of 67.

The benefit one could receive at their full retirement age is their primary insurance amount (PIA). The PIA formula in 2024 has three parts:

1. 90% of the first $1,174 of AIME, plus
2. 32% of any AIME over $1,174 and up through $7,078, plus
3. 15% of any AIME over $7,078

The bend points in the formula above are represented by the figures $1,174 and $7,078. These bend points are adjusted for inflation each year. Since Julie's AIME is less than $7,028, only the first two parts of the formula apply to her. Julie's PIA payable at age 67 would be ($1,174)*90% + ($6,551 - $1,174)*32% or $2,777 monthly after rounding down to the next whole dollar.

If Julie never worked for pay again and collected a Social Security benefit based on her earnings history, she could collect at any age between 62 and 70. Delaying the payment start date past her full retirement age of 67 would increase her benefits. Each month delayed past age 67 up to age 70 would increase the payment by 2/3 of a percent, or 8% per year. If she started payments before her full retirement age of 67, she would see a reduction in her benefits. Working backward from age 67, the reduction is 5/9 of a percent per month for the first 36 months, or 6 2/3 of a percent per year from age 67 to age 64. An additional reduction of 5/12 of a percent per month, or 5% per year, would apply from age 64 to age 62. If Julie claimed her benefit at age 62, she would receive 70% of her PIA or $1,943 per month. At age 70, under the current formula, she would receive 124% of her PIA, or $3,443 per month.

Again, a worker may choose between a monthly benefit derived from their work record or of a spouse or ex-spouse. To collect based on the ex-spouse's earnings, the marriage must have lasted at least 10 years and the beneficiary did not remarry.

This discussion has just introduced you to Social Security and the calculations that apply to most people; it's not a full summary. I recommend *Social Security Made Simple* by Mike Piper for a more in-depth introduction to Social Security. It is an excellent short book that covers more ground than I have here.

CHAPTER 11

Efficiently Withdrawing Your Assets in Retirement

GETTING THE MOST out of retirement assets—whether Social Security or retirement investments—is a goal for everyone. Determining the best age to claim Social Security benefits is a critical component of a well-thought-out withdrawal plan. An introduction to an online retirement calculator sets the stage for this chapter. Then, we'll discuss determining the ideal age to claim Social Security benefits and other factors for your optimal withdrawal plan.

FIRECalc: A Free Online Retirement Calculator

Several free online calculators can aid in retirement planning. The first one I discovered years ago was FIRECalc. I think it's one of the best and it has some unique features I appreciate. As you may recall, FIRE is an acronym: Financial Independence Retire Early. FIRE movement followers seek early retirement, some as young as their 30s or 40s, but you don't need this goal to receive value from this calculator; I continue to use it in my mid-50s. Below is a brief tutorial on FIRECalc. *Nest Egg Care* by Tom Canfield is an additional resource showing how this calculator can help plan for retirement.

About halfway down the right side of the home page of FIRECalc, there is a section that says "Start Here."[36] In this box, you can enter an annual spending rate, the current size of your portfolio, and the number of years you wish your nest egg to last. There are customization options offered in other places.

There are seven tabs on the home page. One is "Other Income/Spending" where you can enter annual Social Security payments in today's dollars for you and your spouse, if applicable, and the start year for those payments. Three adjustments for changes in income or spending can be made at the bottom. For example, you might receive a pension that may or may not grow with inflation, you might pay off a mortgage during retirement, or you might decide to reduce vacation spending after a specific year.

The third tab on the home page, "Not Retired?" allows you to enter the number of years until retirement if you plan to continue working and add an annual amount to your portfolio until retirement. It is assumed that these annual contributions will grow with inflation.

"Spending Models" is the next tab and offers "Manual Entry of Spending Changes," but only to FIRECalc contributors. I donated long before I thought of writing this book since the calculator introduced me to retirement planning and I was grateful for the insight. I use this option in the calculations presented later in this chapter. You may also wish to make a small donation if you feel the same after using FIRECalc.

The "Your Portfolio" tab offers several options. This encompasses specifying both an asset allocation and a portfolio expense ratio. You can choose the method used for calculations as well; one choice relies on past performance, another possibility is to define your portfolio's average rate of return and variability and then generate random results based on these values. You can make up to three one-time changes to your portfolio balance using the "Portfolio Changes" tab, allowing adjustments to your portfolio balance for very large expected expenses or income, such as downsizing to a smaller home, an inheritance, or an expensive dream vacation.

Some of my favorite features of FIRECalc are the options available on the "Investigate" tab. Besides finding "success" and "failure" rates, you can examine how various changes could affect a portfolio's performance. What happens if I change the percentage of stocks in my portfolio? Suppose I postponed retirement for a few more years? What is the highest amount I could have spent to maintain a specific probability of success? If you wish to study the impact of a change in AUM fees, FIRECalc provides options for examining them. The following section explores ways to pick a Social

Security claiming strategy and shows how FIRECalc can examine two or more options.

Ways to Calculate the Best Time to Claim Social Security Benefits

We will examine two of the several ways to estimate the best time to claim Social Security for yourself and a spouse, if married.

Method #1: The Conventional "Break-Even" Calculation

The simplest version of the conventional approach compares any two alternatives. It calculates the number of months of payments it would take before delaying benefits would result in receiving the more significant total lifetime inflation-adjusted benefit. Let's examine Julie's situation introduced in the prior chapter. Julie wants to compare the choice of collecting Social Security at 62 or waiting one year and collecting at age 63. Her projected monthly benefit at age 62, assuming she never works again for pay, is $1,943 in today's dollars; 70% of her PIA of $2,777 rounded down to the next dollar. If she delays receiving benefits for one year, she will receive 75% of her PIA and her payment will increase by $139 to $2,082. She would give up 12 monthly payments of $1,943, or a total of $23,316, by delaying one year. In return, she could receive an extra $139 monthly by delaying claiming her benefit until age 63. If we divide 23,316 by 139, we get between 167 and 168. It would take 14 years of payments (168 months) before delaying payment to age 63 would yield the larger lifetime inflation-adjusted payments. If she wanted to maximize her inflation-adjusted lifetime payments, claiming at age 63 would be better if she thought she would live to at least age 77 (63 + 14). To determine the best overall claiming option, you can compare any period between ages 62 and 70.

I mentioned this is the simplest version of this calculation. A married couple should consider potential survivor benefits, complicating the calculation. If you claim Social Security while still working, the Social Security earnings test may also affect you. In 2024, if you claimed Social Security benefits and were under your full retirement age while earning more than $22,320, the Social Security earnings test withholds $1 of benefits for every $2 in earnings over $22,320. They make an exception for the calendar year a person attains their full retirement age. In 2024, the exemption amount increased to $59,520, with only $1 in $3 withheld.[37] Suppose you are already or will receive a pension and your employer did not contribute to Social Security. In that case, the Windfall Elimination Provision may affect you by reducing benefits. The time value of money is a factor to consider. If you receive money earlier from Social Security, you could invest that money. Typically, even very conservative investments provide a rate of return that exceeds inflation, so a modest discount rate arguably should apply to the cash flows.

It would not be straightforward to consider all these factors simultaneously. Fortunately, there is an online resource that can help: Open Social Security created by Mike Piper.[38] It may be the best free calculator that examines claiming strategies in this manner. It considers all the factors mentioned above and more.

---

37   KA-01921. https://faq.ssa.gov/en-us/Topic/article/KA-01921

38   Free, Open-Source Social Security Calculator. https://opensocialsecurity.com/

Method #2: The Cash Flow Approach

The difference between this method and the one we just discussed is incorporating Social Security cash flows into a cash-flow retirement plan. Let's return to Julie. We ended Chapter 9 with her budget. In today's money, she estimated $75,000 of living expenses per year from age 62 to 65, $69,000 per year from age 65 to 70, $65,000 in her 70s, and $62,000 in her 80s. She also wished to assume five years of long-term care with a life expectancy of 95. In-home care was provided for two years, from 90 to 92 for $95,000 each year. She predicts her last three years will be at a skilled nursing facility costing $130,000 per year. Julie has $1,100,000 in a traditional IRA and her company's 401(k) plan. When she retires, she plans to transfer her 401(k) to her IRA. Julie has a simple 60% stock, 40% bond portfolio she wishes to maintain in retirement, comprising index funds tracking the performance of US stocks and intermediate US Treasuries. Her portfolio's expense ratio is 0.04%. The analysis starts in early 2024 on her 62nd birthday.

FIRECalc can provide some estimates. I start on the home page for FIRECalc, entering the starting portfolio balance of $1,100,000 and 33 complete years for the analysis going to age 95. I skipped the spending section as I provided detailed spending by year in the Spending Model section. In the Other Income/Spending tab, I enter either $23,316 for Social Security starting in 2024 or $41,316 starting in 2032. These figures are Julie's PIA of $2,777 multiplied by 70% and 124%, respectively, rounded down to the next dollar and then multiplied by 12. After that, I entered the spending outlined in the previous paragraph. I selected the total market for her portfolio, with 60% in stocks and 40% in five-year US Treasuries and a 0.04% expense ratio for her index funds.

**Table 11.1 Julie's Retirement Cash Flow Analysis
Start Age 62, Life Expectancy to 95**

	Social Security Claim Age = 62	Social Security Claim Age = 70
Maximum	$6,086,034	$5,723,114
Success Rate	90.8% (109/120)	98.3% (118/120)
Average Final Balance	$1,528,489	$1,694,731
Balance Never Under $250,000	80.8% (97/120)	90.0% (108/120)

Notes:
Calculations performed using FIRECalc (www.firecalc.com)
$1,100,000 beginning portfolio balance at age 62
Investment is 60% stocks / 40% 5-Year US Treasuries, total market (1871-2022)
Social Security is $23,316 per year ($1,943 per month) if claimed at age 62
Social Security is $41,316 per year ($3,443 per month) if claimed at age 70

The results in Table 11.1 are for 120 periods of 33 years from 1871 through 2022. As expected, we get the highest historical return when collecting Social Security earlier. If you knew you would be fortunate, retiring in an environment where the market would give tremendous returns, it would be best to claim Social Security early so you don't have to withdraw as much money from your investment accounts early on. Doing so would allow the investment portfolio to grow more rapidly. We can also see the downside protection that delaying Social Security may provide; the success rate increases from 90.8% to 98.3% when Social Security is delayed until age 70.

Not all failures should be weighed equally. Wouldn't you rather have your portfolio run out of money at age 70 when you began collecting Social Security than at 62? Successes are not all the same either. If your portfolio almost runs out of money before you die, would that cause you anxiety? I know I would have considerable anxiety if that happened to me. One feature in the "Investigate" tab on FIRECalc shows how often a sequence dips below a particular amount. This feature could examine successes with undesirable effects, including possible anxiety. If you wish to ensure your estate receives a minimum amount of money, the "Investigate" tab has an entry for "Leave some money in the portfolio for my estate." Still, as I mentioned, it could also estimate the number of near-failures that could be anxiety-inducing. I entered a value of $250,000 to conduct additional analysis. Claiming Social Security at age 62 resulted in 80.8% of the sequences maintaining a balance of at least $250,000 for the entire sequence. Delaying the Social Security claim age to 70 increased this percentage to 90.0%.

The value to Julie of delaying Social Security to age 70 will depend on several factors. One is life expectancy. In Table 11.1, we are assuming a life expectancy of 95 years, significantly longer than the average woman. Based on the 2021 life tables, the average 62-year-old woman lives an additional 22.1 years, or to age 84.1. Julie wishes to assume a longer-than-average life expectancy but also wants to see the results if she lived to age 90 instead of 95. She keeps five years of long-term care in her spending plan but has those expenses start at age 85 instead of 90.

Table 11.2 Julie's Retirement Cash Flow Analysis
Start Age 62, Life Expectancy to 90

	Social Security Claim Age = 62	Social Security Claim Age = 70
Maximum	$5,157,123	$4,723,444
Success Rate	92.8% (116/125)	97.6% (122/125)
Average Final Balance	$1,387,465	$1,387,799
Balance Never Under $250,000	84.0% (105/125)	91.2% (114/125)

Notes:
Calculations performed using FIRECalc (www.firecalc.com)
$1,100,000 beginning portfolio balance at age 62
Investment is 60% stocks / 40% 5-Year US Treasuries, total market (1871-2022)
Social Security is $23,316 per year ($1,943 per month) if claimed at age 62
Social Security is $41,316 per year ($3,443 per month) if claimed at age 70
Long term care needs begin 5 years earlier than in Table 11.1

The results in Table 11.2 are for 125 periods of 28 years from 1871 through 2022. As expected, there is less of a difference between success rates after the shortened time horizon; it shrank from 7.5% to 4.8%. The success rate is one way to measure the bottom-end protection of a portfolio. An alternative approach is to assess the percentage of time where the balance remains higher than a defined threshold. Again, the gap between the results by claiming age is smaller in Table 11.2 than in Table 11.1. It shrinks from 9.2% to 7.2%.

The relative performance of the age 62 claiming strategy did not just improve when examining downside risk measures. Compared to Table 11.1, there is also a relative improvement for the age 62 claiming strategy in the maximum and average final balance. In Table 11.1, the maximum portfolio ending balance was $362,920, or about 6% less than the age 70 strategy. Shortening the life expectancy by five years increased it to about $433,679, or about 8.4%. Table 11.1 shows that the age 70 claiming strategy produced an average final balance of $166,242 larger than the age 62 strategy does. The difference vanished when the life expectancy decreased to age 90.

There are limitations to free online tools like FIRECalc, such as the number of asset classes considered. However, *Holistic Retirement Planning* uses FIRECalc and calculations from Dr. Damodaran's data to illustrate some of the main investing concepts.

Additional Considerations During Withdrawal

The results above illustrate the concept of a holistic cash-flow calculation. However, the approach is not genuinely holistic; it lacks or glosses over some important details discussed below.

Taxes

Arguably, the biggest weakness with FIRECalc and other free online retirement calculators is the lack of consideration of taxes. The total expenses per year a person places in these calculators assume taxes are one of those expenses. But can you easily estimate your tax expense? You can calculate your tax expense but *evaluating* it can be complex. What does that entail? For Americans, it means examining state and federal income taxes and how they apply to IRAs and the income derived in brokerage accounts through dividends and the sale of investments. Capital gains are taxed differently than ordinary income created by withdrawing money from a traditional IRA. Qualified distributions from a Roth IRA are tax-free and Social Security payments are taxed differently than all other types of income.

Unlike ordinary income, at least 15% of Social Security income is never subject to taxation. As your taxable income rises, a higher portion of your Social Security benefit becomes taxable, reaching a maximum of 85%. The federal marginal tax brackets faced by a retiree receiving Social Security may differ from the ones published by the Internal Revenue Service. The unique taxation of Social Security creates what has been referred to as the Social Security tax torpedo. When income reaches certain thresholds, an additional dollar can cause 85 cents of Social Security benefits to become taxable. So, taking an extra dollar from your IRA could generate an additional $1.85 of your total income to be subject to taxation! For example, a couple in the 22% federal tax bracket may encounter an actual marginal tax bracket of 40.7% (22% multiplied by 1.85). Discussing the details of the Social Security tax torpedo is beyond the scope of this book but to learn more about it, I recommend an article by William Reichenstein and William Meyer in the July 2018 issue of the *Journal of Financial*

Planning "Understanding the Tax Torpedo and Its Implications for Various Retirees".[39]

Roth Conversions

During a Roth IRA conversion, individuals convert some of a traditional IRA to a Roth IRA. In return, the Roth IRA allows the new money to grow tax-free and enables tax-free withdrawals later. We can make Roth conversions during accumulation and later in retirement. They are sometimes part of a strategy to lower lifetime taxes in retirement. Making Roth conversions in years with low reported taxable income can be a savvy move under the right circumstances. When you are in a lower tax bracket than you expect to be in the future, conversions come with a relatively low tax burden up front and can provide tax-free withdrawal in the future. Some retire and delay claiming Social Security, which may offer a chance to change asset location and reduce the impact of the Social Security tax torpedo. Required minimum distributions may force a person to withdraw more money than they need in the future, but for some, Roth conversions can help with this tax hurdle as well. A holistic cash-flow plan considers taxes and the timing and size of any possible Roth conversions.

Creating a Holistic Retirement Cash Flow Plan

Optimizing a retirement withdrawal strategy requires careful consideration of various factors. An optimal plan will include Social Security claiming decisions. If done well, your strategy may reduce the taxes you will pay over your lifetime. It can enhance the likelihood that your

39   July2018_Contribution_Reichenstein.pdf, financialplanningassociation.org

nest egg will last, allow you to increase your retirement budget, or leave a more significant estate to your loved ones. How could one have approached this problem before computer technology? Fortunately, neither you nor I need to dwell on that.

Powerful software can accomplish these things and includes more asset classes. Typically, this software runs analyses called Monte Carlo simulations. They assume an average rate of return for each asset class and a standard deviation measuring variability from the average. The assumptions for average rates of return and variability can be based on historical data or a future forecast. For example, we might assume a mutual fund with a diverse collection of stocks to have an average expected rate of return of 8% with a standard deviation of 17%. About 95% of outcomes fall within two standard deviations of the average. In this example, about 95% of the time, we expect annual returns from this investment between negative 26% and positive 42%. The software can run thousands of simulations for a portfolio based on the averages and standard deviations assumed for each asset class in the portfolio and their relative weights in the portfolio. The reliability of the projections depends on the quality of the underlying assumptions.

New Retirement's PlannerPlus annual subscription of $120 per year at the time of this writing may be well worth the cost for the do-it-yourself investor who is confident in their knowledge base and has read much more than this book on this topic.[40] The full version of the software comes with all these features. In addition, it will allow someone to examine different Social Security claiming ages. It might be the best retirement planning software available for a fee for non-advisors.

40   Pricing | NewRetirement. https://www.newretirement.com/retirement/pricing/

If you hire a financial advisor, consider their fee structure. Is there a potential conflict of interest between your pocketbook and theirs? An advisor working under the popular assets under management model (AUM) may advise their client to claim Social Security benefits at the earliest age possible, age 62. Could this advice impact their pocketbook? Possibly. Following this advice, a client would start receiving money from Social Security as early as possible and would need to withdraw less money from the managed account immediately than if they delayed claiming Social Security. More money in the managed account is more money in the advisor's pocket.

Financial advisors are required to act in the client's best interest, and I suspect most do. However, there could be gray areas involved. What if a client wants to collect Social Security as soon as possible, but the analysis performed by the financial advisor suggests delaying is the better course of action? Even if the advisor conveys this information to the client, how they present it might affect the client's decision. The financial advisor might meet their professional obligation but may not fulfill their moral duty in some people's eyes. I am not saying that financial advisors paid under the AUM model provide lousy advice to line their pockets. All else being equal, I'd prefer a financial advisor to have as few potential conflicts of interest as possible. An advisor charging a flat fee or by the hour may have fewer potential conflicts of interest.

CHAPTER 12

The Investment Policy Statement

AN INVESTMENT POLICY statement (IPS) is a written document that states financial goals. It includes details on implementation, maintenance, and a system for periodic review and potential changes. No plan is perfect and none can guarantee a 100% chance of success. However, the plan should be reasonable and at least come close to reaching the stated goals. When financial advisors create an IPS with their clients, it can include the expectations and responsibilities of both the client and the advisor. What about a do-it-yourself investor? Is there a role for an IPS in their financial plan? Yes. An IPS can be invaluable to someone without a financial advisor. A documented plan is more likely to hold a person accountable than an undocumented one. It can set up rules for investing and changing the investment plan to help avoid behavioral biases and emotions. If we know our potential weaknesses, these rules can be a preemptive strike against our worst tendencies.

Standard Sections Found in an IPS

To some, an IPS can be a simple, no-frills document that covers the basics. Others desire more detail. They may want to explain their decisions and include more information about their plan; it may serve as a reminder in times of market volatility. Detailed explanations can also assist in handling family finances after a death or disability. Following are some sections commonly found in an IPS, but not all investment policy statements require each component and some might include additional sections.

Statement of Goals

An IPS typically begins with a financial goal that should be SMART. If a person in their 20s says they aspire to "accumulate substantial wealth and retire early," this goal is not specific. How much is substantial? Substantial is not measurable. There are no stated means to accomplish their goal. Determining the realism of the goal is challenging due to its ambiguity. The time frame is vague, as "early" means different things to people. To the extent possible, your objectives should adhere to the five traits of a SMART goal. A person decades from retirement may not have an exact dollar amount for their goal, but they can provide more detail than the abovementioned goal There are two examples of an IPS at the end of this chapter; one is for a woman in

THE INVESTMENT POLICY STATEMENT

her 20s just starting a career. I hope her IPS contains a SMARTer goal than our example does.

Statement of Investment Philosophy

Some people choose to state how they invest. This may include statements such as "I am a buy-and-hold investor," "I invest only in low-cost index funds when they are available," or "I do not time the market." These statements may help some in times of market volatility. Further explanations for held beliefs that have influenced your investment philosophy can be included if you think that providing details will help you stay the course or give insight to a disinterested spouse. Just don't make it so long that anyone reading it falls asleep before they finish reading the section.

Present Your Investment Plan to Meet Your Goals

What is the road map to reach your financial goals? Here are most of the major considerations I believe may surface in an IPS.

Asset Choice

This list would include which asset classes to invest in. Your IPS might also state asset classes to avoid and include some that are acceptable but not currently included in the plan.

Asset Allocation and Location/Investment ID

How do we know how much to allocate to each asset class? Determine a percentage weight for each asset class, considering all investment accounts. Some will describe how they arrived at the percentage weights for each asset class. You can list which accounts are suitable for these investments or state the specific investment to represent each asset class.

Investment or Withdrawal Rate

If you are still in the accumulation stage, part of your strategy may be adding additional money to your portfolio. You might add a set amount, like $500 monthly or a percentage of your gross income, to the IPS. During the withdrawal stage, it would provide guidelines on how much money to withdraw.

Statement of Requirements

Some will state requirements for their portfolio, such as that the overall expense ratio for the entire portfolio doesn't exceed a particular percentage. Or there could be a specific waiting period for any proposed change to the IPS to guard against impulsive modifications based on market fluctuations.

Rules for Management

Let's consider additional factors after outlining the plan. How will we manage the portfolio? The percentages assigned to each asset will fluctuate as some perform better than others. What method will rebalance your portfolio to the distribution stated in your IPS? A standard method for rebalancing is when the percentages fall outside an acceptable range. For example, a portfolio consisting of 60% stocks and 40% bonds may allow the asset allocation to fluctuate between 55% and 65% stocks. Once stocks are over 5% from their targeted percentage, the IPS would call for rebalancing the portfolio back to 60/40. An alternative method involves rebalancing at a designated time; quarterly, or perhaps once a year, on your birthday. Your IPS may also provide additional guidelines for rebalancing if doing so may cause a taxable event.

Regardless of the rebalancing system chosen, it's common for an IPS to have a set trigger for its occurrence. The trigger to rebalance could be a calendar date or when the portfolio drifts a specified distance from the stated ideal asset allocation. Setting and following such rules will ensure that market timing is not involved in rebalancing.

Plan for Measurement

It's a normal desire to measure the progress toward your goal and is a yearly commitment for some. Another form of measurement is reviewing the performance of each investment. If you have selected a mutual or exchange-traded fund for your portfolio that claims to track the total US stock market and your investment is in an index fund, you should expect its performance to be similar to the index it claims to follow. Your fund's performance may be slightly less than the index since your fund probably has at least a tiny expense ratio.

Requirements for Modification

Life is full of changes and sometimes there are good reasons to change an IPS. Health issues or losing a spouse can alter your financial priorities. Remember, the personal game plan comes first. Sometimes life does not change but the stock market does. Imagine a market that has been soaring to new heights. There is an emotion—greed—asking us why we have so much money invested in bonds. *I'd be better off if I had only invested more in stocks.* Or perhaps fear kicks in when stocks drop in value by 20%. Hopefully, you contemplated the ups and downs of the market before drafting your IPS and knew the risks and rewards involved.

Two Examples of an Investment Policy Statement

Example 1: Kaitlin, age 23

Kaitlin earned a college degree and recently got a job in her field. She wishes to draft an IPS for the first time. Her parents are successful career professionals who have lived below their means and know the value of investing early. Kaitlin asks for their input while drafting her first IPS. Kaitlin's parents are pleased to help and have a surprise for their daughter: They know she would like to purchase a home and offer her a zero-percent loan for the down payment on a house with repayment due within 10 years. Kaitlin's starting salary is $60,000. Based on her research, her salary is projected to reach $80,000 after three years and $100,000 after 10 years of experience. Kaitlin hasn't decided when she wants to retire or how she'll spend her time in retirement. She wants to be financially independent within 30 years.

Kaitlin's IPS

Goal: To save and invest consistently, reaching financial independence by age 53. I define financial independence as having investment assets equal to at least 30 times my estimated average annual expenses for my life expectancy. My rough estimate in 2024 was $2,250,000 (30 times $75,000).

Investment philosophy: I can't control the market, but I can control expenses. For that reason, I prefer investing in low-cost index funds. If acceptable index funds are not available, I will consider actively managed funds. If I can access low-cost index funds in my employer-provided retirement plan, the expense ratio for my entire investment portfolio should not exceed 0.10%.

Asset choice: Bonds should be in a total US bond market fund with a low expense ratio. Over very long periods, small capitalization value companies have had a higher average rate of return than large companies. Can I expect this to happen in the future? I don't know, but I am young and willing to stick with a slightly overweight portfolio in small-cap value stocks. My asset classes for stocks will comprise the US total stock market, total international stock market, US small-cap value stocks, and foreign small-cap value stocks.

Asset allocation: Bonds will comprise 10% of my investment portfolio until age 40. I will increase this to 20% at age 40, 25% at age 45, and 30% at age 50, which will remain for the rest of my life. I will maintain a portfolio of 70% stocks after age 50 because of my above-average risk tolerance and the need for growth if I retire around the age of 53. If I keep working after achieving financial independence, my need to take risks will decrease, and I might consider increasing my bond holdings. For the stock portion of my portfolio, I wish to have 80% in US stocks and 20% in international stocks. I also can have up to 20% of my stocks in funds for small-cap value companies; half in US companies and half in foreign companies. My desired asset allocation in 2024 was 10% of the total US bond market, 63% of the total US stock market, 9% of US small-cap value stocks, 9% of the total international stock market, and 9% of foreign small-cap value stocks.

Asset location: My employer provides options to contribute to a 401(k) and a Roth 401(k). I already have a small amount of money in a Roth IRA and may consider opening a traditional IRA. Each year, I will decide what percentage of my contributions will be after-tax, Roth, or traditional by considering the marginal federal tax brackets and comparing them to my salary minus the standard deduction for the year. In 2024, after taking the standard deduction, the last dollar I earned would still be in the 12% marginal tax bracket. For 2024, all my contributions were to Roth accounts. In future years, for income in the 22% tax bracket, my contributions will be 25% Roth and 75% traditional. Above the 22% bracket, all contributions will be traditional. If tax rates change in the future, I will update this IPS and place all bonds in traditional accounts first. Small-cap value funds in my employer plan are limited and have very high costs. I will make these investments in my traditional and Roth IRA accounts.

Contribution rate: I plan to contribute 20% of my gross income to my traditional and Roth investment accounts. Including my 5% employer match, this is a 25% contribution rate. After repaying the loan from my parents, I plan to increase my contribution rate by 5% to help limit lifestyle creep.

Maintenance: I will rebalance my total investments to my global asset allocation at the end of each year when I also record the change in my net worth.

Modifications: After a one-month waiting period, modifications can be made to this IPS.

Example 2: Bill and Kim, both age 64

Bill and Kim are nearing 65 and plan to retire together. Early in their working lives, they only invested enough in their respective employer 401(k) plans to get the employer match. In their late 40s, they realized the need to increase their contribution rate to have the type of retirement they desired. Since they were in a high-income bracket, they invested all this money in traditional IRAs and 401(k)s. About six years ago, their youngest child moved out and became self-sufficient so they increased their savings rate again. Besides contributing the maximum amount allowed to their IRAs and 401(k) plans, they made significant contributions to a new brokerage account. Bill and Kim already have an IPS, but the goal was attaining enough invested assets to feel comfortable retiring at age 65. Having accomplished their goal, they seek to create a new IPS to prepare for retirement this year.

Kim manages the family's finances, which is just fine with Bill. She has taken a great interest in personal finance and has become quite knowledgeable. Bill has much less interest in and knowledge of personal finance than his wife. They do not use a regular investment advisor but Kim sees the value of using an "advice-only" advisor who charges a flat fee or by the hour. Kim believes getting a second opinion on their family plan from a professional would be prudent if she continues to manage the family finances herself in retirement.

Bill and Kim's IPS

Goal: We want our investment portfolio to support us for 30 years, until age 95, as we make withdrawals based on our budget. We will use various strategies outlined in this document to maximize the likelihood of reaching this goal.

Our investments: We are fans of Vanguard and their low-cost index funds. Our portfolio comprises 60% stocks, 40% bonds, and a money market account with six months' expenses. Vanguard's total US stock market ETF is 75% of our stock holdings (45% of our portfolio). We divide the remaining 25% of our stock holdings (15% of our portfolio) into two index funds. Two-thirds of our investment is in Vanguard's total international stock ETF. This ETF has only about 4% invested in small foreign companies. By comparison, about 8% of the US market comprises small companies. The performance of small-cap foreign companies is somewhat less correlated with the US market than the global world market, excluding the US. We choose to over-weight small foreign companies and they represent one-third of our foreign stock holdings (5% of our portfolio). Inflation concerns us, so half of our bonds are in TIPS (Treasury inflation-protected securities). The other half is in intermediate US government treasuries. We desire to maintain this portfolio for life.

Asset location: At age 65, we will have three investment accounts: Bill's traditional IRA, Kim's traditional IRA, and a brokerage account. At age 65, the brokerage account will represent about 15% of our total investment portfolio. This brokerage account has one fund, the tax-efficient total US stock market index fund. It should remain the only fund in this account. Tax-free rebalancing will occur within the traditional IRAs. If we convert some of our traditional IRAs to a Roth IRA, the bonds will stay in the traditional IRAs if possible; they will only be placed in a Roth IRA if the traditional IRAs represent less than 40% of our total investment portfolio.

Strategy: We will continue using the retirement planning software Kim purchased. Our plan calls for both of us to delay claiming Social Security until age 70. To minimize expected lifetime tax payments, the software recommends Roth conversions before age 70. The software will update our goal's "probability of success" as our time horizon shortens and our account balances fluctuate. We want this probability to remain close to 95%, but we know it will change, especially if there is a significant drop in the stock market. Although the plan is designed to withstand market declines, we are implementing additional measures for peace of mind. A considerable portion of our budget is for discretionary spending. If the "probability of success" at the end of the year is between 80% and 90%, we will only spend 50% of our budgeted discretionary spending in the next calendar year. If it goes below 80%, we will only spend 25% of our discretionary spending in the next calendar year. We will allow a one-time 10% increase in the discretionary budget if we reach a 98% success rate by year-end.

Additional rules: Rebalance the overall portfolio at the end of the year. The IPS has a one-month waiting period to incorporate any changes. Any significant changes in the IPS should consider consulting with an "advice-only" advisor.

Contingency plan: If Kim can no longer manage the retirement portfolio due to her passing or signs of cognitive decline, someone else will need to take over, but it should not be Bill. After much research, Kim has developed a Plan B: A financial advisory firm with a holistic approach to retirement planning. This firm uses the AUM compensation model, but the AUM fee is about half of what an average advisor charges and its approach to retirement planning is similar to Kim's. Bill has the firm's information in case he ever needs to use it.

CHAPTER 13

—

An Introduction to Estate Planning

WHAT IS YOUR first thought when you hear the word "estate"? People often associate it with immense wealth. For that reason, some may think estate planning is only relevant for the affluent. But it is not.

What makes up a person's estate? An individual's estate includes all their rights, interests, or titles to any property. Property can take several forms. Homes and the land they sit on are real property. Additionally, it covers tangible assets such as cars and collectibles, and intangible assets like mutual funds held in an IRA.

This chapter discusses some common objectives of estate planning, how an estate is distributed, considerations before creating an estate plan, and the relevance of some common estate planning documents.

Common Estate Planning Objectives

Estate plans can have different objectives, but there are commonly shared objectives. To understand the importance of estate planning, let's start by discussing some goals that a good estate plan can achieve.

Providing for the Financial Needs of Survivors

This first one is obvious. If we have loved ones who need or would benefit from the financial resources in our estate, we want to get these resources to them efficiently—both in the speed of delivery and the minimization of expenses involved, including fees and taxes.

Distributing Assets According to Your Wishes

This does not just pertain to assets with significant financial value. Have you considered sentimental items with little monetary worth? Loved ones fight over such things while they are still grieving their loss. Perhaps you know of a few special items your children might desire. Consider addressing these items in a will so your loved ones know your desires; it may also prevent rifts in your loved ones' relationships from developing or growing deeper.

Reducing the Burden on Your Family

Often, a close family member handles the estate of a loved one who has passed and they too will probably experience a period of grief. Making the process as easy as possible is likely to be appreciated. Knowing you cared enough to plan to make things easier for them may be the last way you show your love for them.

Protecting from Creditors

Estate plans should be constructed with intention. You may build them to limit creditors' access. An estate planning professional can provide guidance on this and many other issues.

Planning for Incapacity

Estate planning is not just for our eventual death, it also prepares us for the possibility of becoming incapable of making thoughtful decisions later in life. Choosing who you wish to decide on your behalf if you become incapacitated is an integral part of estate planning. Deciding how much power to give them is also essential.

Transferring a Business

Do you own a business? If so, consider how you wish to transfer your ownership interest.

Avoiding Probate

Probate is one way an estate is distributed but there are several potential drawbacks to doing so. We discuss probate in more detail in the next section.

How Estates Are Distributed

One critical decision to make with an estate plan is how your assets will be distributed—inside or outside of probate.

Inside Probate

Probate is a legal process of validating a will (if one exists) and distributing property according to the will. A will is a legally enforceable declaration of how an individual's property, subject to probate, should be distributed after death. A mentally competent person can always revoke or amend a will.

A person who dies without a will dies "intestate." When this happens, state intestacy laws determine the distribution of assets through the probate process. For example, a state law may first allocate all assets to a surviving spouse. If there is none, they may divide all assets among any children of the decedent. The state establishes rules based on how most people want their assets distributed and must guess the decedent's wishes since they did not leave a valid will.

Outside Probate

Ways to transfer estate assets after death outside of a will are sometimes called will substitutes. Will substitutes include beneficiary designations on life insurance policies, IRAs, annuities, and pensions. Bank accounts provide for transfer with payable-on-death (POD) accounts. A similar type of transfer can occur with brokerage accounts, which have transfer-on-death (TOD) accounts. Some kinds of property are also transferred outside of probate based on the type of ownership, such as joint tenancy with the right of survivorship and tenancy by the entirety.

Most trusts are also will substitutes. A trust is a legally enforceable arrangement involving a grantor (the person creating the trust), a trustee, and a beneficiary. The grantor transfers the property to the trustee, who becomes the legal owner. The trustee manages the property and then gives it to the beneficiary. Only a testamentary trust established within a will undergoes probate.

Reasons to Avoid Probate

Let's examine a few of the most common reasons why many want to avoid probate.

Time

A critical element of efficient distribution is quickly transferring your estate to the desired beneficiary. Probate can be a lengthy legal process, taking months—and sometimes even years—to complete. A will substitute can be more efficient. Efficient, timely distribution of assets may reduce stress for your loved ones, something that goes beyond just their financial value.

Cost

Probate is a legal process, and as such, it involves court and attorney fees. These fees can be significant and reduce the beneficiary's eventual benefit.

Lack of Privacy

The probate process is legal and part of the public record. Do you wish to keep your financial matters private? The distribution of assets through will substitutes keeps things confidential.

Multi-State Probate

What happens if you die owning homes in two different states? If your estate properties go through probate, two processes would occur, one in each state. Holding the properties in a living trust could avoid a multi-state probate.

Protection from Creditor Claims

The probate process requires creditors to be notified. As a result, an estate handled in probate may be more likely to receive claims from creditors.

Reasons to Choose Probate

The list above may lead one to believe that probate should always be avoided. However, it is essential to consider some beneficial aspects of probate.

Validation of the Will

People challenge their loved one's wills on certain occasions. Having a legal process to deal with these issues may be beneficial.

Fraud Protection

As stated earlier, probate is a legal process open to public view. This may make fraud less likely, and court oversight may increase scrutiny of any questionable activity.

Protection from Creditor Claims

Wait! I thought this was a reason for avoiding probate. It is. As with many things, one should consider the pros and cons. In probate, creditors must provide evidence. The structure and oversight of the probate process are essential considerations.

Should I Create a Trust?

As mentioned earlier, the distribution of a trust not created inside a will occurs outside of probate. The probate-or-no-probate decision is just one consideration; there are others beyond the ones already mentioned. Trusts may be preferable if you have a complex estate or want more control over your assets. Trusts can address charitable giving, unique wishes, and special needs.

In a trust, someone can establish an income and remainder beneficiary. One party, the *income* beneficiary, receives income from a trust over their lifetime for a specified period. Upon their death or elapse of the specified period, the *remainder* beneficiary (or beneficiaries) take ownership of the assets. Picture a woman who has a daughter and two grandchildren. She might consider establishing her grandchildren as remainder beneficiaries, allowing her daughter to receive income from the trust over her lifetime. This type of trust is called a generation-skipping trust (GST). A GST is a tool to control the timing and level of support provided to the ones you love.

Some wealthy parents with affluent children have used this technique to help limit their children's tax burden when they pass away and escape estate taxes for multiple generations. In response, the Revenue Act of 1976 established the Generation-Skipping Transfer Tax (GSTT). However, this tax only applies to estates worth many millions of dollars.

It is also possible to create a particular type of trust where the remainder beneficiary is a charitable organization. These trusts are called charitable remainder trusts (CRT). The income beneficiary in these trusts is often a non-charitable beneficiary, such as a surviving spouse who receives income for a specified period, often for life. After that, ownership transfers from the trustee to the charitable organization.

If you or a loved one you wish to provide for in your estate has special needs or a disability, look into a special needs trust (SNT). There are two general types of SNTs. Someone, not the beneficiary, often a close family member such as a parent or grandparent, creates a third-party SNT. Since the assets of these trusts are not considered assets of the beneficiary, they can receive income from the trust without jeopardizing their eligibility for means-tested government benefits, such as Supplemental Security Income (SSI) or Medicaid. A special needs trust funded by the beneficiary's assets is a self-settled or first-party SNT. These assets may include an award or settlement in a personal injury lawsuit or an inheritance. This type of SNT can also help persons with special needs or disabilities receive income without the risk of losing key government benefits. These types of trusts are complex and require special attention. An experienced estate attorney familiar with special needs trusts should be involved with creating and regularly reviewing an SNT.

Estate Planning and Taxes

Part of the efficient distribution to a beneficiary considers taxation, but you don't have to wait until you die to transfer some of your assets. Consider taking tax-savvy actions before passing. One such activity is gifting—transferring something of value with a present interest that the recipient can immediately use or appreciate. If you forgive a debt, it is considered a gift. If you sell your child a used car for $3,000 but it is worth $15,000, you have given them a $12,000 gift. In 2024, a person could provide gifts of up to $18,000 per recipient without paying a gift tax. Married couples could split gifts, granting up to $36,000 per recipient in 2024. The gift tax rule excludes payments for educational and medical expenses provided they are paid directly to the institution. If you give the money to the beneficiary and *they* pay the institution, it is considered a gift payment subject to possible gift taxes. Pay the institution directly. One more thing: Direct payments from a noncustodial parent can, under some circumstances, impact the eligibility for financial aid. Please do your due diligence to ensure your actions don't have any unforeseen negative consequences.

Consider the following example. Your daughter got married in 2024. The newlyweds aim to save for a down payment on a home within two years. You wish to help them out and have the means to do so. The plan is to give your daughter $20,000 to put toward this goal. You and your spouse could each give a cash gift of $10,000 in 2024, but you think of a better plan. Years ago, you purchased individual stocks in a brokerage account. One purchase was for a company called Apple. You invested $1,000 in Apple, which is now worth $12,000. You will gift your investment in Apple stock to your daughter in 2024.

What happens if your daughter sells her holding in Apple in 2024? She would inherit the original cost basis of $1,000, so $11,000 plus any additional appreciation (or depreciation) in value by the time of sale would be subject to capital gains taxes. The time clock for the period the stock was held was also inherited by your daughter. Since you held the stock for more than one year before gifting it, she could sell it immediately and be taxed at long-term capital gains rates. In 2024, a married couple's 0% federal tax bracket for long-term capital gains goes up to $94,050, and the standard deduction is $29,200 for couples filing jointly. If your daughter sells the stock in 2024, the newlyweds will pay no federal capital gains taxes if their total income, including the capital gains, is less than $94,050 plus $29,200, or $123,250. You knew their income in 2024 would place them in the 0% tax bracket for long-term capital gains and advise your daughter to sell her gift immediately. Your gift to them was as good as $12,000 in cash, and you received a personal bonus: you avoided paying capital gains taxes on your investment in Apple. You will consider gifting approximately $8,000 in highly appreciated stock holdings in your brokerage account next year after ensuring they would be in the 0% tax bracket for long-term capital gains. If they are not, giving cash is always an option.

The discussion above only considers federal income taxes. State income taxes may still apply. In this example, the parents could gift additional cash to cover any state income taxes; state taxes would be less than the capital gains taxes they would have paid if they sold their holdings in Apple stock.

Assets in a brokerage account get a step up in cost basis for the beneficiary, either at the time of death or six months after death if the estate chooses the "alternative valuation date." However, in the example above, the recipient could receive the financial support earlier, free of any federal taxation, when they could use it. You also gain personal satisfaction by witnessing the money used while you're still alive. Gifting can be an attractive way to transfer some of your wealth before death if it does not endanger your nest egg's ability to provide for your future needs.

Married people typically name their spouse as their beneficiary. What happens when the first spouse passes away? The marital deduction allows for an unlimited transfer of assets from one spouse to another over a lifetime. This effectively defers any federal estate taxes until the second spouse passes away.

Only the very affluent would pay federal estate taxes at that time. In 2024, the applicable exclusion amount was $13,610,000 for all money gifted before death or transferred after death as part of the estate. So, estates with less than $13.61 million in assets and previously gifted assets would pay no estate taxes. In addition, when the first spouse dies, any unused applicable exclusion amount is portable and transferred to the second spouse. The applicable exclusion amount will be reduced at the end of 2025 per a 2017 Tax Cuts and Jobs Act provision, but few individuals possess estates of such high value.

Careful tax planning should consider more than just federal estate taxes, it should also consider any tax issues the beneficiary might face after receiving their inheritance. These include state estate and inheritance taxes, which differ by state. Certain states exempt estates from taxation, while others have varying exemptions and rates. It may be prudent to get the advice of a knowledgeable professional.

Here's one more tax-related thought to ponder: When the first spouse passes away, changes often affect the federal taxes of the surviving spouse. If they filed jointly as a married couple using the standard deduction, that deduction is reduced for a new filing status. If they both received Social Security benefits, the surviving spouse only receives the more considerable benefit of the two in the future. Changes in income streams and the size of standard deductions affect taxes for most people. A holistic retirement plan can consider these issues, but the timing of when they will happen is still being determined. Once the unknown becomes known, the plan can be changed accordingly. The death of a spouse does not just raise estate issues, it often calls for an updated holistic retirement plan.

Planning Your Estate

I have provided a general overview of some crucial issues in the estate planning process, but it is not comprehensive. I intend it to provoke intentional thought about estate planning and hit some key points. With this in mind, we now turn to a five-step process for completing an estate plan.

Step 1: Examine Your Net Worth

Hopefully, you are already tracking your net worth. If not, estate planning is a reason to start. Take inventory of what you have before considering how to distribute it. As a reminder, net worth is simply the value of your assets minus your liabilities. Your assets include money or holdings in retirement, checking, savings, and brokerage accounts. It includes life insurance policies, annuities, real estate, and personal property. If you have an ownership interest in a business, it is also one of your assets. Your liabilities include any unpaid debt, such as credit card balances and the amount needed to pay off a home mortgage or car loan.

Step 2: Decide Who Gets What and Identify Any Special Circumstance

Here, you decide who gets what. However, this step involves more than that: Do you wish to avoid probate to keep your affairs private?

Do you want to plan for a disabled spouse or child who will need special care after your death? Do you have any plans for a particular charity or a loved one? Consider not only tax consequences for the estate but also for the recipient. After all, you want your loved ones to get as much use as possible from the assets you can pass on to them.

Step 3: Determine the Structure of Your Plan

This is where you decide the best way to achieve the objectives laid out in Step 2, such as the costs and benefits of various potential alternatives: *Should a trust be a part of my estate plan? How much of my net worth will already be transferred by other will substitutes such as designated beneficiaries on IRAs, checking accounts, etc.? Are there any ways to structure my estate plan to save taxes? Should I transfer some of my assets to loved ones while I am still alive or would such moves jeopardize my retirement nest egg over my lifetime?* I recommend seeking the advice of an estate planning attorney and a financial advisor well-versed in estate planning issues when deciding on the structure of your plan.

Step 4: Create the Documentation

Estate planning involves creating documents to ensure your wishes are carried out. Each plan is unique, but here are five of the most common documents found in an estate plan:

Last Will and Testament

This is the place to start. A will is a legally enforceable document that conveys your wishes. In it, you designate the individuals who receive your possessions. As mentioned earlier, this may include sentimental items of little monetary value. If you expect loved ones to question your decisions, you can provide explanations for clarity. You can also name guardians for children or pets in a will.

Living Will

Also known as an advanced health care directive, a living will convey your preferences for life-sustaining treatments and end-of-life care if you cannot make them. Family members may disagree with your wishes, but putting them in a living will ensure they are enforced and respected.

Health Care Power of Attorney (POA)

A health care power of attorney is someone you entrust to make medical decisions for you if you cannot do so. The scope here is broader than that of a living will; it can include surgeries and treatments that are not life-sustaining or involve end-of-life care. Having a health care POA can be crucial in unforeseen medical situations.

Durable Power of Attorney (POA)

In this document, you authorize a person you trust to make personal, financial, and business decisions on your behalf. A person given just "power of attorney," or non-durable POA, loses their ability to make these decisions on your behalf if you become incapacitated. Therefore, a durable POA is often preferable.

Revocable Living Trust

This is probably the most common type of trust. The revocable nature allows you to make changes as your life situation changes and you can maintain control of the trust by naming yourself the trustee. We have discussed only a few of the many desirable attributes of trusts. Seek legal advice when considering the formation of a trust.

Step 5: Review and Monitor

With most plans, periodic review is essential. Any life changes may generate a change in the estate plan you desire. It is also a good idea to ensure your beneficiaries are up-to-date and reflect your wishes; some have accidentally left their ex-spouse as a beneficiary.

—

CHAPTER 14

Getting Help

ONE GOAL OF this book was to help readers become better-informed consumers of financial services. Some wish to pass as much control as possible of managing their financial assets to a financial advisor. Many need to learn what a financial advisor does. Others must know about their service charges. I understand why this happens—they are not interested in managing their nest egg because they think they lack sufficient knowledge to do the job well and see the process as too complicated. They want someone else to deal with it and believe a professional will do better than they could. However, this begs a few questions: *Who do I trust to manage all my financial assets? Do I know what services they provide? How does it compare to other advisors? How do the costs for their services measure up to other alternatives?* It's vital to understand the services provided and their actual costs when getting help to manage your finances.

How should you think about seeking help? First, you must know about the services that may be valuable to you.

Potentially Desired Services

Below are eight retirement planning services some may desire from a financial advisor.

Portfolio Construction

Your portfolio needs to be built with your objectives and risk tolerance in mind, including asset allocation and location. You may handle everything else yourself if you are willing and competent enough to manage the portfolio. But many prudent do-it-yourself investors hire a financial advisor at either an hourly or flat-fee rate to critique a portfolio they consider implementing. The cost for such a review can be worthwhile.

Systematic Rebalancing

You chose your asset allocation for a reason. Rebalancing prevents your portfolio from drifting too far away from your target allocation. If you have a systematic approach to rebalancing, it will limit the potential impact of behavioral biases and the temptation to time the market. Rebalancing in a tax-advantaged account, like an IRA or company-provided 401(k), does not trigger a taxable event. Consider tax implications if rebalancing involves buying and selling in a brokerage account. To rebalance with tax-advantaged accounts, you need to calculate the amount of your holdings to purchase or sell.

While this may be tedious, systematic rebalancing is arguably the most straightforward service of the eight on this list to do yourself.

Opportunistic Tax Loss/Gain Harvesting and Roth Conversions

The market can change unexpectedly. Tax-savvy moves, such as tax loss or gain harvesting, may be worth considering when there are large swings in the market. A Roth conversion may also be worth considering if your income drops and you are in a low tax bracket. Do you want a financial advisor to help determine the right move for you when the unexpected happens?

Plan for Non-Retirement Goals

This book has focused on retirement planning but there are other forms of financial planning. For example, you might wish to fund a child's college education and need guidance on achieving this goal.

Social Security and Pension Optimization

Social Security optimization is *not* collecting the most you can from it over your lifetime. Your tax liability depends on your Social Security income and other income. Making the Social Security decision without considering your other income sources may lead to a less-than-optimal choice. If you hire someone to help determine the best time to claim your Social Security benefit, ask them how they make that determination. If they do not consider your other income sources in their determination, I would ask why. We have not discussed pensions, but the same considerations apply. Pensions often offer the choice between a lump-sum payment and monthly payments. It makes sense to see how the options measure up in a tax-efficient cash-flow retirement plan.

Health Care Planning

People often need to seek health coverage after retirement from a full-time job. If you live in the United States and are under 65, you must decide on the best choice for you. When you reach 65, you need to determine your desired Medicare coverage. Then there is the elephant in the room: long-term care is costly in the United States, so what is your plan to pay for it? Consider consulting a financial advisor or professional versed in health care insurance options.

Legacy Planning

Do you want help to plan your legacy? This might involve hiring an estate attorney, a financial advisor, or both. A financial advisor may design a retirement plan to leave beneficiaries with a specified amount of assets.

Tax-Efficient Retirement Cash Flow Plan

A tax-efficient retirement cash-flow plan can include many considerations, such as stress tests. A financial advisor should perform some stress tests that may include longevity, high levels of inflation, or market returns well below average. If you have any specific areas of concern, will they include those in their stress tests? Does the plan include considerations for tax hurdles, such as the Social Security tax torpedo and required minimum distributions? What about state subsidies for the Affordable Care Act and IRMAA fees once you reach 65?

Things to Know About Financial Advisors

We now have a list of services we might wish a financial advisor to perform for us, depending on the price. Let's focus on financial advisors' compensation, work models, and the two advisor types.

Financial Advisor Compensation

You walk into a fine steakhouse, are seated, and a server hands you a menu. When you open it, you notice there are no prices. *Wow, this place must be expensive! They don't want to show me their prices. It doesn't even say "market price" next to the entrees.* Next, you observe other customers all have big stacks of documents sitting on their tables. What is going on? You ask the server and he says, "Oh, the prices depend on your net worth. We review everyone's net worth at AUM Steakhouse; the more your net worth, the more your entrée costs."

Sounds absurd? However, the assets under management model of compensation for financial advisors is a bit like this steakhouse experience. Many financial advisors using this model charge 1% of AUM up to the first $1 million they manage. If you need $300,000 of assets managed this year, it will cost you $3,000. What if your assets are worth $600,000? Oh, that will be $6,000. You ask, *Does managing $600,000 worth of assets require more advanced skills than managing $300,000? Does it require twice the time?* Do you hear the crickets?

Some financial advisors charge a flat or hourly fee for their services. Their payment does not depend on the amount of money at stake. As you might have guessed, I generally prefer this compensation model. However, in some circumstances, the AUM model may provide good value for a financial services consumer. We discuss choices later in this chapter.

Financial Advisor Model

There is more to consider than how a financial advisor is compensated; another critical issue is whether the client is the sole source of compensation for the advisor. A fee-based advisor may receive commissions for selling financial products or securities to their clients, which could create a potential conflict of interest: If the advisor promotes a product, they will receive a commission for selling it. Does that commission impact the advice they are providing? Clients often view a fee-only advisor as a better fit because of this concern. The client is the only one compensating the advisor, providing more transparency between them. Just be aware that potential conflicts of interest can still exist with a fee-only compensation model. For example, an advisor paid by AUM may advise a client to claim Social Security as early as possible, requiring less immediate withdrawals from the assets managed because Social Security provides some income.

Many in the financial services industry paint the fee-only model as the gold standard for minimizing potential conflicts of interest. I'm afraid I must disagree. An advice-only compensation model, where the client is the only one who compensates the financial advisor, is arguably a better model to minimize potential conflicts of interest. If someone pays an advisor a flat fee for a specified service or by the hour for advice, what incentive would the advisor have to give anything less than their best advice? The only cynical response I can come up with would be if the advisor were to purposely suggest a more complicated solution than needed to increase their billable hours.

I believe the advice-only model is generally the most transparent and least susceptible to conflicts of interest.

Two General Types of Financial Advisors

There used to be just one type of advisor: human. But technology has now brought us an additional option, the robo-advisor. A robo-advisor offers an automated, algorithm-driven approach to wealth management. Those willing to forgo the personal touch of a traditional human advisor typically pay much lower service fees. Two popular robo-advisors are Wealthfront and Betterment. Wealthfront charges an AUM fee of 0.25% to manage an account. Betterment also charges a 0.25% AUM fee for account management for balances over $20,000 or accounts with reoccurring monthly deposits of at least $250. Services at both Betterment and Wealthfront include portfolio creation, tax loss harvesting, and rebalancing.

Charging about 25% of a typical human advisor's AUM fees, a robo-advisor may be an attractive option for those wishing to have someone else manage their financial assets. However, there are some downsides to using a robo-advisor. Many people value the personal touch of a human advisor who can discuss and understand their client's situation. Also, there are some things a robo-advisor will not do, such as determine an optimal cash-flow retirement plan that includes selecting a claiming strategy for Social Security income.

The Real Cost of Advice

The financial cost of advice is not simply the cost per year. If you spend $3,000 on financial advice in a year, the immediate impact on your bottom line is $3,000 less in assets. However, you forever lose that $3,000 and any compound growth it could have generated. The actual cost of financial advice includes the impact of advisor fees on the likelihood that you will reach your goal. It also consists of the reduction in the size of your estate created by these costs.

Let's use FIRECalc one last time to measure the actual financial cost of advice. In this example, we will use the data from 1871 through 2022 for our calculations. Consider someone with $725,000 in assets to be managed, invested 60% in stocks (total market) and 40% bonds (five-year US Treasury) with an expense ratio of 0.05%. The goal is to withdraw an inflation-adjusted $30,000 for 25 years without running out of money. Payments start at the beginning of 2024 and run through 2048 (yes, people generally have a more complicated portfolio, but the focus here is only on the cost of advice for a given portfolio). Consider the cost of advice for four people using different portfolio management approaches for the same portfolio.

Diane uses a pure DYI approach with a $200 per year cost for software to aid in managing her portfolio. Her total cost is $200 annually, plus the 0.05% expense ratio. The second person is also a DIY investor. Courtney takes Diane's approach and seeks annual hourly advice for four hours at $250. Courtney's costs are $1,200 per year in today's dollars, including the same financial planning software, plus the 0.05% expense ratio. The last two people hand their portfolios to a financial advisor who charges a percentage of assets managed. Beth shopped around and found an advisor who provided all the services she desired and more with a below-average AUM fee of 0.50%. Including investment fees, Beth's total cost is 0.55% of assets managed. James uses the services of a family friend who charges a typical 1% AUM fee. Including the expense ratio for his investments, the total cost for James is 1.05% of assets managed.

Let's compare the results for Diane, Courtney, Beth, and James based on the 128 time periods with a 25-year duration from 1871 through 2022. The maximum final balance was

- ➜ $3,109,613 for Diane
- ➜ $3,043,614 for Courtney
- ➜ $2,689,062 for Beth
- ➜ $2,307,186 for James

The success rates for Diane, Courtney, Beth, and James were 99.2%, 96.9%, 96.9%, and 93.0%, respectively. Their average final balances were $992,990, $939,478, $820,202, and $660,454. Remember, all the results are inflation-adjusted. The actual monetary differences with inflation would be more significant. I also checked the percentage of sequences where the balance always remained above $200,000. The following were the success rates for each: 89.1%, 85.9%, 78.9%, and 73.4%.

Fees matter a lot. That's the point. You may find the difference in results for a 0.5% AUM fee versus a 1% AUM fee to be eye-opening. Beth and James had an average difference in the final balance of nearly $160,000. Some people spend hours deciding which smartphone, computer, or large-screen TV to purchase but hardly any time choosing their financial advisor and could save tens (if not hundreds) of thousands of dollars by finding an advisor with lower fees offering the same services. Cost should not be the only consideration when deciding on financial advice, however, it is crucial to understand the actual lifetime costs for each option you are contemplating. They can be substantial!

An Additional Online Calculator

Other free online calculators may be of interest. One is cFIREsim (cFIREsim), which uses data dating back to 1871. I especially appreciate two of its features. One is the statistical summary provided for each analysis. In addition to the average outcome, cFIREsim reports each analysis's median, 10th, and 5th percentile. The other nice feature is that this calculator allows users to customize income and spending by year with the "Add Adjustment" feature. If you wish to perform a similar analysis for Diane, Courtney, Beth, and James in cFIREsim to examine results at the 50th, 10th, and 5th percentiles, please note that cFIREsim uses the 10-year US Treasury for bonds. FIRECalc offers more than this one option for bonds, but the 10-Year US Treasury is not one of them.

What are some of cFIREsim's limitations? Like FIRECalc, cFIREsim does not consider taxes. This calculator also offers a smaller set of asset classes to choose from than FIRECalc and lacks the handy features found in the "Investigate" tab on FIRECalc.

Where to Find Professional Help

Where can you turn for low-cost financial advice from a human advisor? Several websites may be worth visiting: Advice-Only Financial is run by Harry Sit.[41] He offers a directory of advice-only advisors meeting specific criteria. You may find other valuable information on his website even if you wish to avoid paying for access to his directory.

Advice-Only Network provides a free directory of advice-only financial advisors.[42] Not all people in this directory offer low-cost options for financial advice. Using this website involves separating the wheat from the chaff, but there might be a suitable choice for you here.

Finally, Sara Grillo compiled a list of low-cost advisors in 2022; depending on your situation and needs, the options may be of interest.[43]

If you pursue a free consultation from a firm, remember to determine your costs under their compensation model. If their website is transparent about fees, you should know their costs before speaking with them. If you have questions, inquire about their methods and philosophy before deciding whether their services meet your needs.

---

41   Advice-Only Financial, adviceonlyfinancial.com

42   adviceonlynetwork.com

43   https://saragrillo.com/2022/05/16/list-of-low-cost-financial-advisors/

The Sales Pitch?

I've read quite a few books on retirement planning. I enjoyed one of them until I reached the end when I received a last-minute sales pitch. That left me feeling very disappointed.

This is not one of those books. I do not work as a financial advisor. The companies, services, or products I have mentioned in a positive light may be helpful to some readers. At the time of this writing, I have no professional connection to anyone or any business mentioned in *Holistic Retirement Planning*.

But I do have one request for you: Getting noticed is challenging for new authors so it would mean a lot to me if you left an honest review of *Holistic Retirement Planning* at your place of purchase, on Goodreads, or BookBub. I promise to read your reviews and appreciate your time in writing them. Below is a QR code and a web link to the review page for my book on Amazon.

https://www.amazon.com/dp/B0DFMW25P5/

Thank you for reading *Holistic Retirement Planning*. We all aim for maximum life fulfillment and that involves making prudent financial decisions. However, we should never forget that financial resources have no intrinsic value. Aligning these resources with your values, interests, and goals gives them real value.

Best wishes for putting together a holistic retirement plan that is right for you.

Index

C

F

G

H

P

payable on death (POD) accounts 186

pay-yourself-first budgeting 48

philosophy 171

Piper, Mike 152, 159

portfolios. *See* investment portfolios

poverty level, federal 123

power of attorney (POA) 196

probate 186–188

R

real estate 97

recency bias 21, 30, 36

reflection 15–17

Reichenstein, William 164

required minimum distributions (RMDs) 115

retirement planning. *See also* Social Security

  accumulation phase 65, 75–78, 84, 88, 92

  activities, hobbies 15, 109, 112

  budgeting 110–114, 136–137

  contributions 41, 58, 63, 98

  financial services 200–201

  forced income 115–118

  4% rule 67, 81

  holistic retirement planning 118, 163, 165–166, 193

  housing, residency 113–114

  IRAs 62, 98, 99, 115, 116–118, 125

W

Y

Z

Printed in the USA
CPSIA information can be obtained
at www.ICGtesting.com
JSHW052321190924
70068JS00003B/10